THE MORAL
TEACHING
OF PAUL

THE MORAL TEACHING OF PAUL

SELECTED ISSUES

3RD EDITION

VICTOR PAUL FURNISH

Abingdon Press
Nashville

THE MORAL TEACHING OF PAUL
SELECTED ISSUES, THIRD EDITION

Copyright © 1979, 1985, 2009 by Abingdon Press

All rights reserved.

This book is printed on acid-free paper.

Library of Congress Cataloging-in-Publication Data

Furnish, Victor Paul.
    The moral teaching of Paul : selected issues / Victor Paul Furnish.—
3rd ed.
        p.   cm.
    Includes bibliographical references and index.
    ISBN 978-0-687-33293-9 (binding: pbk., adhesive perfect : alk. paper) 1.
Ethics in the Bible.   2. Bible. N.T. Epistles of Paul—Criticism,
interpretation, etc.   I. Title.

BS2655.E8F79   2009
241'.0412092—dc22   2008053598

09 10 11 12 13 14 15 16 17 18—10 9 8 7 6 5 4 3 2

MANUFACTURED IN THE UNITED STATES OF AMERICA

To

Dorothy Jean Furnish

Sister

Colleague

Friend

CONTENTS

PREFACE TO THE THIRD EDITION

It has been exactly thirty years since the original edition of this book was published, and almost twenty-five years since the appearance of the second, revised edition. While the second edition was but a modest revision of the first, this third edition is a thoroughgoing revision of the second. In preparing it, I have sought to take account of the many important contributions that have been made to Pauline studies, including and especially Pauline ethics, over the years since the earlier editions were published. My aim has been to enrich the discussions of the selected topics by paying closer attention to the sociocultural context of Paul's ministry, the complexity of his thought, the character of his moral reasoning, and the way his thought and reasoning may inform and challenge our own. *Quote this in summary.*

Although chapter 1 has been trimmed down in some respects, it has also been augmented with further comments about the differences between Paul's world and ours. Chapters 2, 3, and 4 have been substantially rewritten, and chapter 5 is entirely new. Chapter 2 now includes a section on Paul's references to sexual immorality, more detail concerning marriage and divorce laws and customs in the Greco-Roman era, and additional remarks about the character of Paul's counsels in 1 Cor 7. In chapter 3, more attention is given to the Levitical prohibition of same-sex intercourse, there is now a discussion of the Genesis creation accounts, and there is more documentation of first-century attitudes

1

toward homoerotic conduct and the presuppositions that engendered them. In chapter 4, the discussion of the baptismal affirmation in Gal 3 has been expanded, and my reading of 1 Cor 11:3-16 is, I trust, more carefully and cogently presented. Chapter 5, which now deals with Christians in society, replaces a chapter in the first two editions that dealt with the more restricted issue of Christians and the political order. This new chapter has been adapted, with the permission of the publisher, from my longer, more detailed study, "Uncommon Love and the Common Good: Christians as Citizens in the Letters of Paul," in *In Search of the Common Good* (Theology for the Twenty-first Century, ed. Patrick D. Miller and Dennis P. McCann; New York and London: T & T Clark, 2005), 58–87.

Preface to the Second Edition

A number of important studies of particular aspects of Paul's moral teaching have appeared since the first edition of this book was published, and I have sought to take account of these as I have prepared this revision. My fundamental conclusions about Paul's views on the issues considered here remain essentially unaltered, but I have changed my mind about some specific matters. Therefore, while there are alterations of various kinds throughout this new edition, no chapter has been completely rewritten. There have been some additions, however, and certain sections have been completely rewritten, especially those that deal with 1 Cor 7:10-11, 1 Cor 6:9, and 1 Cor 11:2-16, in chapters 2, 3, and 4, respectively.

Some notion of my indebtedness to other scholars can be gained from the bibliographical sections at the end of each chapter, each of which has been brought up-to-date. I wish to record as well my appreciation to those reviewers of the first edition who raised important questions or made constructive suggestions. Not least, it is a pleasure to acknowledge how much I have gained from the many opportunities I have had to discuss the chapters with lay and clergy groups. These experiences have suggested that this little book has indeed been found helpful by many who (as I wrote in the preface to the first edition) "believe that Paul's moral teaching ought to be taken seriously but who are not sure what it means to do so."

PREFACE TO THE FIRST EDITION

This book is written for people who believe that Paul's moral teaching ought to be taken seriously but who are not sure what it means to do so. I have outlined my own convictions about this in chapter 1. In the subsequent chapters, I have sought to demonstrate how some problem texts in Paul's letters can still give moral guidance in our time if we do not force our presuppositions and questions upon them too quickly.

I was encouraged to move ahead with the publication of these short studies by the need, expressed to me often by laypeople, clergy, and students, for sound, but nontechnical, discussions of these problem texts and topics in Paul's letters. It is for such readers that this book is intended. Several of the chapters have been shaped in no small part by opportunities I have had to discuss these issues in the seminary classroom, at pastors' conferences, and in local churches. Many technical matters have been omitted from the presentation; others have been greatly simplified but, I hope, not misrepresented. The books and articles referred to at the end of each chapter will provide additional information and in certain cases different opinions.

The writing of this book was worked into a schedule that my wife and daughters thought was already too crowded, and without their understanding and support it could not have been accomplished. The manuscript was typed by Mrs. Bonnie Jordan with her usual skill and efficiency.

A Note on English Versions of the Bible

Scripture quotations, except as noted, are from the New Revised Standard Version of the Bible, copyright 1989 by the Division of Christian Education of the National Council of Churches of Christ in the USA. The following abbreviations have been used in citing English versions of the Bible:

ASV	American Standard Version
CEV	Contemporary English Version
JB	Jerusalem Bible
KJV	King James Version
NAB	New American Bible
NEB	New English Bible
NIV	New International Version
NJB	New Jerusalem Bible
NRSV	New Revised Standard Version
NTPIV	The New Testament and Psalms Inclusive Version
REB	Revised English Bible
RSV	Revised Standard Version
TEV	Today's English Version

CHAPTER 1

THE SACRED COW AND THE WHITE ELEPHANT

The Apostle Paul is doubtless one of history's most controversial and misunderstood figures. His dramatic and unexpected conversion—from being a zealous Pharisee who persecuted the church to claiming that he had been authorized as an apostle of Christ—not only alienated him from his former colleagues in Judaism but also made him immediately suspect even within some Christian circles. Subsequently, as his mission to the Gentiles took on momentum and gained in significance, his dealings with the venerable and venerated leaders of the Jewish-Christian congregations in Judea became increasingly tense and difficult. To his Gentile converts, as well, he often posed a puzzle. How, for example, could he declare (as in Rom) that belonging to Christ both frees one from the law and claims one totally to obey the will of God? Or how could he say (as in Phil) that believers have important worldly responsibilities, even though their true citizenship is in heaven?

In the late nineteenth and early twentieth centuries many Protestants, especially, took a dim view of Paul's theological claims. Some charged that the apostle had corrupted the "religion of Jesus" into a "religion about Jesus" by imposing concepts and practices drawn from Greek and Roman religions. Others argued that he had imposed on it the burden of rabbinic concerns and methods. In Germany, William Wrede (1859–1906) spoke for many when he identified Paul as "the second founder of Christianity," and lamented that, while Jesus' teaching had exerted "the better" influence on Christianity, Paul's had exerted "the stronger."

More recent studies of Christian origins have shown that it was quite mistaken to label Paul the founder of Christianity, as we know it. He was converted by and into a Christian movement that already had a rich theological tradition and that already had been nurtured by various religious and cultural sources. Although he made his own important theological contributions, the church was neither "founded" nor "refounded" on his doctrines. Its foundation was in the "Easter faith" of Jesus' earliest followers—their experience that the crucified one lived among them still, as the risen Lord.

The old complaint about Paul's theological doctrines has, in our day, been replaced in part by complaints about his ethical appeals and directives. Many readers find them to be arbitrary and expressed in an authoritarian way. It is true that the apostle was often bold and blunt in the directions he gave, the advice he offered, and the opinions he expressed. Moreover, much of his moral teaching seems completely removed from twenty-first-century realities and concerns. His general appeals present no special problem; it is easy to agree that we should "pursue love" (1 Cor 14:1), "bear one another's burdens" (Gal 6:2), and "hold fast to what is good; abstain from every form of evil" (1 Thess 5:21b-22). Yet we begin to have problems whenever Paul's admonitions become specific and concrete, as they so often do: men should not wear long hair (1 Cor 11:14), while women should (1 Cor 11:15);

one should not use the secular courts (1 Cor 6:1-11); one should accept the social status in which one finds oneself (e.g., slavery, 1 Cor 7:17-24); it is better to remain single than to marry (1 Cor 7:7a); and many more. How are we to understand these concrete instructions? In what way, if at all, can they help us think through the moral issues with which we are confronted today?

Where Do We Find Paul?

Anyone who attempts to understand Paul, whether it be his life, his ministry, or his thought, must begin by making some decisions about sources. The earliest and most important evidence for understanding who he was and what he thought is provided by the New Testament—above all in Paul's letters, and secondarily in the book of Acts. There are no Christian or non-Christian sources for Paul's life and thought that are as early or as valuable as these.

Since the second century, church tradition has attributed the writing of both the book of Acts and the third gospel to Luke, whom Paul identifies as one of his "fellow workers" (Phlm 24). Although there is no question that Luke and Acts constitute a single, two-volume work produced by one person, whether that person was Luke is quite uncertain. Even if the tradition is right about this, however, the accounts of Paul's ministry and especially of his preaching disclose primarily the author's views, not those of the apostle himself. Thus, as helpful as Acts is concerning aspects of Paul's travels, it offers little help concerning his theological stance or concrete moral instruction.

Our most valuable sources for Paul's preaching and teaching are his own letters. Seven of the thirteen New Testament writings that bear his name can be accepted with confidence as his. In their present canonical order, these are Romans (Rom), 1 and 2 Corinthians (1, 2 Cor),

Galatians (Gal), Philippians (Phil), 1 Thessalonians (1 Thess), and Philemon (Phlm). We may think of these as the undisputed letters.

The other six New Testament writings that bear Paul's name are often called deutero-Pauline because, while they show the influence of Paul's thought, their authenticity is at least doubtful. In canonical order, these are Ephesians (Eph), Colossians (Col), 2 Thessalonians (2 Thess), 1 and 2 Timothy (1, 2 Tim), and Titus. Ordinarily, scholars attribute these six disputed letters to at least four writers and date them (variously) to the decades following Paul's death, from as early as the 70s to as late as the first decade of the second century. Those who judge these letters to be deutero-Pauline often describe them as attempts of later writers to interpret and apply the apostle's teaching to needs and situations that he himself had not confronted and could not have foreseen. Opinions vary on how well these interpreters did their job and on how much they may have altered, whether intentionally or unintentionally, Paul's actual views. (See further, "The Problem of Sources" in ch. 4.)

In this and the following chapters we must give our chief attention to the seven letters of undisputed Pauline authorship. It is in them that we shall find the apostle, to the extent that he discloses himself to us; and it is in them that his thought will be most accessible to us if we pay careful attention.

What Do We Do with Paul?

Locating the writings in which Paul and his thought are most accessible is only the first step. The second is to try to *understand* what he was aiming to communicate in his letters. Doing this is not a simple task. It requires knowledge of the circumstances that occasioned each letter, an awareness of the broader historical and cultural contexts of Paul's ministry, and an appreciation of his Hellenistic-Jewish heritage—to mention just a few examples. But while Pauline scholars will continue to differ on various points of interpretation, understanding Paul is by no means a hopeless task. There is, in fact, no other first-century Christian about whom we can know as much as we know about this apostle, and no other whose thought we can understand as fully.

But understanding Paul is one thing, and deciding "what to do" with him is another. At the very least, he is to be acknowledged as a seminal figure in the history of Christianity and, therefore, a person of considerable consequence in the development of Western civilization. Moreover, from the second century forward the Christian community has accorded his letters scriptural status, viewing them as, in some respect, authoritative for its faith and life. It is necessary to include here the qualifying phrase *in some respect* because there are, in fact, different views of *how* Scripture is authoritative, and each of these has particular consequences for how we assess Paul's concrete moral advice and instruction. At the risk of caricature but for the sake of clarity, we may contrast two very different ways that his concrete moral teaching has been approached. There are some who venerate it as a sacred cow and others who dismiss it as a white elephant. As each of these positions is characterized and the errors in each identified, it will become clear that the approach in the following chapters can be identified with neither.

Paul's Moral Teaching as a Sacred Cow

Some people believe or at least read the Bible as though they believe that Scripture is the written deposit of God's revealed truth, mediated through inspired writers in centuries past but valid in both general and specific ways for all times and places. I am calling this the sacred-cow view of the Bible. It leads to the conclusion, when applied to the concrete ethical teachings of Paul, that they are, in fact, God's commandments and thus eternally and universally binding. They are not to be touched, disturbed, or in any sense explained away. They are to be taken at face value. Proponents of this view of the Bible often cite 2 Tim 3:16-17, which refers to Scripture as "inspired by God." This is offered as "proof" that the teachings of the Bible are of divine origin exclusively and, therefore, in no way conditioned by the cultural setting of the biblical writers. It would seem to follow, then, that if we are uncomfortable with what Paul says—for example, about slaves, women, or civil authorities—that is our problem, not the Bible's. If Paul's words are really God's words, then Christians have no business trying to accommodate them to modern views or sensibilities. Rather, Christians must accommodate *themselves* by obeying the apostle's teachings as the universally and eternally binding commandments of God.

The fundamental problem with this way of approaching the Bible, including Paul's moral instruction, is that such an approach seriously misrepresents the understanding and intentions of the biblical writers themselves. It is true that the Hebrew prophets, for example, had uttered their oracles as spokesmen for God. But it is also true that those same prophets were conveying God's word for particular situations, and that they understood it to be addressed to people who lived within a specific span of time and a particular geographical area. Neither they nor those who later compiled their oracles and committed them to writing presumed that the prophets' words could be isolated from the particularities of the situations in which they were originally spoken.

But then what of the statement in 2 Tim 3:16-17 that is so often quoted in defense of a sacred-cow conception of the Bible? (Most scholars today attribute 2 Tim and the other so-called Pastoral Epistles—1 Tim and Titus—to an anonymous Christian of the late first or early second century.) In Greek, the opening words of verse 16 are grammatically ambiguous. Is the writer claiming that "all scripture is inspired by God and is useful" (NRSV) or that "every scripture inspired by God is also useful" (NRSV alternative translation)? In either case, the primary claim is about the *function* of Scripture: that it is useful "for teaching, for reproof, for correction, and for training in righteousness, so that everyone who belongs to God may be proficient, equipped for every good work." By "scripture" this writer probably means, as Paul had, only the *Jewish* Scripture, which Christians commonly refer to as the Old Testament. The description of Scripture as "inspired by God" (literally, "God-breathed") calls attention to its divine origin and, hence, its authority. But in and of itself, this description says only that the biblical writers were in some way moved and guided by God. It does not identify their words as God's own words. People who interpret the expression to mean "historically accurate," "inerrant," or the like impose their own ideas on the text. To accept the Bible as in some way "inspired" does not require us to think of it as infallible, entirely unaffected by the cultural settings in which the writers labored, wholly consistent, or unconditionally binding for all times and in all situations.

This idea is confirmed with special clarity in the instance of the Pauline letters. The apostle understood himself to be an interpreter of Scripture, not one of its authors. He could not have imagined that his letters would in time be reckoned as part of Scripture. His aim in writing was to address the particular needs of specific Christian congregations, in specific locations, involved in specific situations, at specific times. Since we are not the readers whom Paul had in mind, we must *interpret* his letters, including his moral instructions. They are by no means automatically and entirely applicable to us in our situations. We may speak of Paul's ministry, and therefore of his teaching, as "inspired," but this does not alter the fact that his words were directed to first-century people and situations, and that what was pertinent in their times and places may not be in ours.

The New Testament scholar Willi Marxsen (1919–1993) illustrated this point in the following way. Suppose that Paul dictated his letters to the churches in Galatia and Thessalonica on the same day (although this was not actually the case). And suppose further that when his scribe addressed the apostle's letters for delivery, he mistakenly wrote "To the Thessalonians" on the one bound for Galatia and "To the Galatians" on the one bound for Thessalonica. What would have happened when the Thessalonians, between whom and Paul there were strong and mutual bonds of love and affection, opened up the letter addressed to them and found the angry and sarcastic words intended for the Galatians? And what would have happened when the Galatians discovered that they had mistakenly received Paul's letter to the Thessalonians? Now, certainly, the Thessalonian and Galatian Christians had much more in common with each other than twenty-first-century Christians have with either. Yet even in the Galatian churches and in the church at Thessalonica some careful interpretive work would have been required in order to make those misdelivered letters intelligible and meaningful. How much more are we in the position of needing to *interpret* Paul's letters precisely because they were not intended for us but for others!

Interpretation is rendered all the more important because the social, cultural, and political contexts and circumstances of the apostle's first-century congregations were vastly different from the contexts and circumstances of Christian congregations today. Our world is different from theirs; the challenges and opportunities of our times are in significant respects different from the challenges and opportunities that they faced. As a result, what made Paul's letters intensely relevant for those to whom they were addressed makes them problematic for us. Here one sees in operation what I have ventured to call *the law of diminishing relevancy:* to the extent that something is specifically appropriate in one particular situation, it is less specifically appropriate in any and every other particular situation. We must keep this in mind, especially when considering Paul's moral advice and directives.

There is yet another reason why one must avoid turning the apostle's moral teaching into a sacred cow. Paul himself allows for differing ethical judgments, given the differing circumstances of individuals even within the same congregation and at the same time. He sometimes shows a remarkable tolerance of rather differing behavior within the Christian communities. He accepts the fact, even affirms it, that some Christians will eat meat that has been ritually slaughtered in a pagan temple, while others will feel bound to abstain from it. He allows that some Christians will marry, while others will remain single; that some will divorce, while others will maintain their marriages, and so forth. Some of these points will be examined in more detail later on. Here it is enough to emphasize that Paul nowhere lays down a rigid, legalistic code of Christian conduct. Taking his moral teaching as a sacred cow, therefore, simply will not work.

Paul's Moral Teaching as a White Elephant

If, as suggested, the sacred-cow interpretation of Paul's ethical teachings is not in accord with the apostle's intentions, is our only alternative to dismiss them as constituting a bulky white elephant? We often apply this image to possessions or ideas that have turned out to be useless and without value (any neighborhood garage sale offers numerous examples). According to some, although Paul's moral teaching may have been valuable in other times and circumstances, it is now obsolete, a curious relic of the past that does not address current issues or meet present needs.

Those who dismiss Paul's moral teaching as a white elephant typically argue that he regarded it as provisional, intended only for the time that remained—which he supposed would be relatively short—before the Lord's return and God's final victory over sin and death. And further, that moral instructions conveyed under those circumstances cannot possibly be relevant in a world whose continuing existence shows that Paul was mistaken, and whose moral challenges are in many ways different and vastly more complex. This point of view deserves careful examination and response.

Early in the twentieth century, the influential New Testament scholar Martin Dibelius (1883–1947) argued that belief in the imminent return of Christ and inception of God's reign precluded any *principled* concern for a "Christian ethic." According to him, the moral appeals that Paul and others found it necessary to issue in the meantime had been largely recycled from Jewish and other, Hellenistic sources, although "christian-ized" as needed. Thus, in Dibelius's view those appeals had "nothing to do with the theoretic foundations of the ethics of the apostle, and very little with other ideas peculiar to him. Rather, they belonged to tradition." That is, in his concrete instructions Paul was dependent on the traditions of the church, which had, in turn, been adapted from non-Christian sources. In preaching to converts from a Gentile background, Christian missionaries like Paul found it necessary to convey such basic moral instruction for purely practical reasons, not because it was related in any essential way to the proclamation of the gospel. So the ethical sections of Paul's letters, Dibelius held, are there only because of Paul's "didactic habit" of giving ethical instructions to new converts. In this view, the Pauline ethical teaching is not only unrelated in any significant way to Pauline theology; it is, in fact, seen as having existed in spite of the early church's expectation that Christ would soon return, bringing in the king-dom of God. So we have been left with a white elephant.

A similar conclusion was reached about a decade later by Albert Schweitzer (1875–1965), but in a different way. He argued that Paul's theology is oriented fundamentally to the idea of a "mystical" dying and rising with Christ. The apostle's ethical teaching was developed, then, "solely from the character of the new state of existence which results from the dying and rising again with Christ and the bestowal of the Spirit." Schweitzer acknowledged that Paul regarded the end of history and of the world as imminent, and for this reason, he said, the idea of a coming judgment and reward still lingers in Paul's ethical teachings. Yet the essential character of Paul's ethics does not derive from the apostle's expectation of the coming end of the natural world; its *essential* character derives, instead, from the experience of being in Christ. Thus, for Schweitzer, Paul's mysticism was more important than his eschatology (his expectations concerning the end time) and saved him from denying the world in the way that most first-century Christians did. The "ideal of Paul's ethic," he wrote, was "to live with the eyes fixed upon eternity, while standing firmly upon the solid ground of reality." In effect, Schweitzer was suggesting that Paul's ethical teaching is better than one might suppose it could be, considering his sense of standing near the close of history. The apostle's eschatological doctrine was, in effect, "trumped" by his mysticism. While Schweitzer admired Paul's ethical teaching, he nonetheless regarded it as existing *in spite of* the apostle's eschatology.

More recently, the views of Dibelius and Schweitzer have been echoed in part by Jack T. Sanders, an American New Testament scholar. Like them, Sanders argues that Paul's belief in the shortness of time left for this world precluded his developing any significant ethical teachings for life in the world. He believes that Paul was correct in identifying love (*agapē*) as the power of the "new existence," but he holds that because the apostle viewed this new existence as fulfilled only in the future, the love command does not apply to the present. According to Sanders, this meant that when Paul was faced with the necessity of issuing moral directives, he had to fall back on arbitrary legalisms, sayings of Jesus, or ad hoc revelations from the Lord. In this reading of Paul, his concrete moral instructions again turn out looking very much like a white elephant, a burdensome possession that has little or no present value.

At first, it may seem more reasonable to set aside Paul's moral teachings as a white elephant than to venerate them as a sacred cow. Such a view has the support of some respected scholars, and it certainly avoids the error of interpreting timely instructions as if they had been offered as timeless truths. But this white-elephant interpretation too is involved in a fundamental error. The evidence of Paul's letters suggests that his eschatological outlook did not diminish but, in fact, reinforced his concern to provide moral instruction that was in accord with the gospel he preached.

The arguments of Dibelius and others, that first Jesus and then the post-Easter church more or less perfunctorily espoused Jewish or Hellenistic, or Hellenistic-Jewish, morality and traditions, do not do justice to the evidence. Jesus' preaching of the nearness of the reign of God did not preclude or cause the subordination of practical ethical concerns. In fact, it accentuated the sovereignty and scope of God's claim. Jesus' ministry of compassion, love, and service within the family of God is integrally related to his eschatological message about the imminence of the kingdom. Its nearness brings a new urgency to the ethical appeal. Similarly, the so-called ethical sections of the apostle's letters are not loosely tacked on to the weightier, theological parts as concessions to the practical needs of the less-than-ideal Christians in Paul's congregations (Dibelius). Rather, Paul's ethical admonitions are closely and significantly related to his preaching of the gospel, and thus to his fundamental theological convictions. What matters most, he insists, is *faith enacted in love* (see Gal 5:6) in the present life of the believer and of the believing community. In one way or another, most of the apostle's concrete moral instructions are intended to show the forms that faith's enactment in love must take in specific cases.

It is true that Paul does occasionally issue more or less arbitrary pronouncements on matters of behavior, what Sanders (following Ernst Käsemann, 1906–1998) calls "tenets of holy law." These usually involve some warning about the visitation of God's judgment upon those who fail to keep them. In such pronouncements—which, however, are neither as numerous nor as arbitrary as Sanders suggests—one can detect the influence of traditional modes of exhortation (e.g., 1 Cor 3:17). But these statements should not be isolated from the wider context of Paul's ethical teaching. They are only elements embedded within larger units of teaching, and a fair appraisal of the relation between eschatology and ethics in Paul's thought can only result when the broader contexts are considered.

First Thessalonians, probably the earliest of Paul's surviving letters, offers a good illustration of the way his eschatological outlook *supports* his ethical appeals. In chapters 4 and 5 the apostle is assuring the Thessalonian Christians that the members of their church who have died before the Lord's return will by no means miss out on the end-time events. He declares that the dead will be resurrected and, together with those who remain alive, will be taken up to be with the Lord forever (4:13-17). Underlying this hope is the community's belief that Jesus himself "died and rose again"; it is, indeed, "through" the resurrected Jesus that God will bring the dead to life, that they may share in the coming salvation (4:14). In other words, for Paul the *decisive* eschatological event has occurred already in the death and resurrection of Christ (see also 5:10). For this reason, Paul believes that, however long or short the interval before the Lord returns (he discourages speculation about this, 5:1-3), the *present* has already been graced and claimed by God.

This explains why, in contrast to the Jewish traditions on which he draws, Paul offers relatively little detail about the anticipated end-time events. He emphasizes, rather, the saving power of Christ's death and resurrection (4:14; 5:9-10), that those who belong to the Lord are "children of light and children of the day" (5:5), and that faith and love, along with hope, are the distinguishing hallmarks of Christian existence (5:8). He therefore does not call on believers just to *wait passively* for the dawning of the end time. Because they already "belong to the day" (5:8), they are both required and empowered to take up the distinctive armor of faith, love, and hope (see also 1 Thess 1:3).

This idea of the present as already claimed and qualified by the future can be traced throughout Paul's letters. Romans, perhaps the latest of those that have survived, offers an especially important example. There, eschatological references both open and close a long section of moral appeals and exhortations. Introducing them, Paul urges, "Do not be conformed to this world, but be transformed" (12:2). And concluding them, using expressions reminiscent of 1 Thess 5, he solemnly declares that "the night is far gone, the day is near. Let us then lay aside the works of darkness and put on the armor of light; let us live honorably as in the day, not in reveling and drunkenness, not in debauchery and licentiousness, not in quarreling and jealousy," and so on (13:12-13). In fact, every major block of practical appeals in the Pauline letters is specifically and emphatically supported with references to the hope by and in which believers live, and by and in which they have been granted a new identity "in Christ."

The Role of the Spirit

The relationship between the apostle's eschatological outlook and his concrete moral instructions may be further clarified by noting how he views the Holy Spirit. He regards the Spirit of God as the manifestation of God's empowering presence both in the life of the believing community and in the lives of individual believers. We often use spatial terminology when thinking and speaking of God and the Spirit—for example, God is "up there" and sends the Spirit "down here" to dwell among us and in our hearts. Paul too sometimes uses spatial language of this sort when speaking of the Spirit's powerful, abiding presence (e.g., in Gal 4:6). But to specify the larger significance of the Spirit's presence, he employs two striking *temporal* metaphors.

One of these metaphors derives from the Festival of the Harvest (or of Weeks) that was observed in ancient Israel. During this annual celebration, the first and presumed choicest portion of the season's harvest was offered in thanksgiving to God. These *firstfruits* were not the whole, but they represented and in an important sense embodied the whole, symbolizing that the entire harvest was God's gift. So when Paul describes believers as those "who have the first fruits of the Spirit" (Rom 8:23), he is claiming that through the Spirit's presence, the saving power of God is already at work, even in the midst of the present age, confirming believers in their hope (vv. 24-25) for the full harvest (the "glory" of life with Christ, vv. 17, 18, 21, 30) that is yet to come.

Elsewhere, using a metaphor that derives from the world of business and commerce, Paul describes the Spirit as a *down payment* or *first installment.* In one instance the reference is to the Spirit's dwelling with the apostle himself: "It is God who establishes us with you in Christ and has anointed us, by putting his seal on us and giving us his Spirit in our hearts as a first installment" (2 Cor 1:21-22). Later in the same letter, using the same Greek expression, the reference is to God's bestowal of the Spirit on the whole believing community: "God . . . has given us the Spirit as a [first installment]" (2 Cor 5:5 NRSV, with my alteration). Such "earnest money" is not the entire sum, but it represents the whole and establishes the credit of the one from whom it has come. In both instances Paul is thinking of the gift of the Spirit as the effective presence of God's power in the present—not the fullness of it, but no less the reality of it in the believer's life. This image, like that of the "first fruits," shows that the concept of the Spirit plays a key role in Paul's thinking about the present and the future. Through the Spirit, the power of the coming age—God's saving power—is already at work in the present.

What has this to do with ethics? How does this conception help us understand the vital relationship that exists between Paul's eschatological expectation and his concrete moral instructions? The answer is clear when we recognize that for Paul the power of the coming age is the power of *love*, and not just love in general but God's love: the love through which God has created all that is, in which God wills that it be sustained, and by which God acts to redeem it. Paul identifies Christ's death as the definitive manifestation of this love, the event by which the world is freed from the power of sin and reconciled to God (Rom 5:6-11; 2 Cor 5:14-20). This is the love—*God's* love—by which faith is simultaneously engendered and empowered to express itself in the believer's life (Gal 5:6, where the form of the verb [NRSV alternative translation: "made effective"] suggests that Paul views faith as rendered active by God's love and expressed in the believer's love).

Even as Paul regards Christ's death as the event by which God's love is established, so also he thinks of the Spirit as the decisive *bearer* of God's love, the means by which that love is given a vital presence in the believer's life. "God's love has been poured into our hearts through the Holy Spirit that has been given to us," and it is for this reason that "hope does not disappoint us" (Rom 5:5). Paul then proceeds to identify Christ's death as definitive of God's unconditional, self-giving, others-regarding love: he died for us "while we were still weak . . . ungodly . . . [and] sinners" (Rom 5:6-8). This is the kind of love to which the apostle has reference when he advises the Galatian Christians that while we are waiting for the "hope of righteousness," nothing else really matters except "faith made effective through love" (Gal 5:5-6).

Concluding Observations

It is unacceptable to treat Paul's moral instructions as if they were a sacred cow, and equally unacceptable to treat them as if they were a white elephant. It is not just that these approaches are too extreme, requiring us to look for some middle way. Rather, they are both wrong. The one approach, for which the sacred cow has been our symbol, misunderstands the nature of the Bible, the intentions of the biblical writers themselves, and the ways in which the moral instructions of Paul are related to the specific needs of Christians living in the Greco-Roman world. The other approach, symbolized here by the white elephant, fails to perceive the close relationship that exists between Paul's proclamation of the gospel, including his eschatological outlook, and his concrete ethical teachings and exhortations. Consequently, before the meaning of Paul's moral teaching for our day can be determined, its meaning for and in Paul's own day must be assessed. This requires that we pay attention both to the sociopolitical context of the apostle's ministry and to the character and content of his proclamation as a whole.

One final observation about sacred cows and white elephants may help to clarify what is being proposed here. *Whenever we treat Paul's moral teaching as if it were a sacred cow, we run the risk of turning it into a white elephant.* That is, if we regard the particulars of Paul's moral instructions as automatically applicable and binding in our times and circumstances, we will almost certainly end up with a good many requirements that are either irrelevant or, what is worse, clearly inappropriate.

No doubt, a number of moral issues taken up in the Bible have modern counterparts; for example, the plight of those who suffer, who have been marginalized by society, or who are otherwise disadvantaged; dishonesty in the marketplace; the breakdown of domestic relationships; problematic sexual conduct; the administration of justice; and the hostility of social and political institutions or forces toward people of faith. Yet to some degree, every one of these issues has a *different* character today. An immense gulf exists between the particular circumstances and conditions that gave rise to these issues in ancient society, and formed the contexts in which they had to be addressed, and the circumstances and conditions that obtain for us.

For the same reason, we will find nothing in Paul's letters, or anywhere in the Bible, about certain moral issues that the modern world dare not ignore: the proliferation of nuclear, biological, and chemical weapons; the threat of overpopulation; the fact of global warming; the pollution and exploitation of this planet's natural resources; international terrorism; terroristic nationalisms; the moral challenges raised by developments in genetic engineering and medical science; economic imperialisms; and the increasing gap between rich nations and poor nations.

Finally, then, we need to remember that even though there are topics, like those chosen for discussion in the following chapters, that are in some respect common to the apostle's day and ours, Paul's moral teaching was addressed to the situations that confronted him, not to those that confront us. Moreover, it is equally important to recognize that we have access to knowledge (e.g., about the physical world) and resources (e.g., social, political, and religious) for addressing moral issues that could not have been imagined by the apostle or his contemporaries. Our task, therefore, is not to search the Pauline letters for ready-made answers to the moral questions that confront us. It is, rather, to consider whether, and if so, how Paul's approach to the moral issues specific to *his* day may inform and guide us in thinking through the moral issues that are specific to our times and places.

For Further Reading

Books mentioned or quoted in this chapter: William Wrede, *Paul* (London: Green, 1907; 1st German ed., 1904), especially 179, 180; Willi Marxsen, *The*

New Testament as the Church's Book (Philadelphia: Fortress, 1972; 1st German ed., 1966), 152; Martin Dibelius, *From Tradition to Gospel* (London: Nicholson and Watson, 1934; 1st German ed., 1919), especially 238–39; Albert Schweitzer, *The Mysticism of Paul the Apostle* (2nd ed.; London: Black, 1953; 1st German ed., 1930), especially 297, 311, 333; Jack T. Sanders, *Ethics in the New Testament* (Philadelphia: Fortress, 1975), chapter 3.

General introductions to Paul and his thought: Morna D. Hooker, *Paul: A Short Introduction* (Oxford: Oneworld, 2003); David G. Horrell, *An Introduction to the Study of Paul* (Continuum Biblical Studies; London and New York: Continuum, 2000); Leander E. Keck, *Paul and His Letters* (2nd ed.; Proclamation Commentaries; Philadelphia: Fortress, 1988). More detailed: Udo Schnelle, *Apostle Paul: His Life and Theology* (Grand Rapids: Baker, 2005; German, 2003).

Other presentations of Paul's ethical outlook: Victor Paul Furnish, *The Love Command in the New Testament* (Nashville: Abingdon Press, 1972), chapter 3; Richard B. Hays, *The Moral Vision of the New Testament: Community, Cross, New Creation: A Contemporary Introduction to New Testament Ethics* (San Francisco: HarperSanFrancisco, 1996), chapter 1; Willi Marxsen, *New Testament Foundations for Christian Ethics* (Minneapolis: Fortress, 1993; German, 1989), 142–227; J. Paul Sampley, *Walking between the Times: Paul's Moral Reasoning* (Minneapolis: Fortress, 1991). More detailed: Victor Paul Furnish, *Theology and Ethics in Paul* (Nashville and New York: Abingdon Press, 1968; reissued in the "New Testament Library" series, Louisville: Westminster John Knox, 2009); David G. Horrell, *Solidarity and Difference: A Contemporary Reading of Paul's Ethics* (London and New York: T & T Clark, 2005).

For excellent discussions of the letters widely regarded as deutero-Pauline, see Raymond F. Collins, *Letters That Paul Did Not Write: The Epistle to the Hebrews and the Pauline Pseudepigrapha* (Good News Studies 28; Wilmington, Del.: Glazier, 1988).

CHAPTER 2

SEX, MARRIAGE, AND DIVORCE

We know from Paul's letters that some of his converts were upset or at least confused by certain statements that he had made about sex, and therefore in doubt about his attitudes toward marriage and divorce. Despite the apostle's attempts to explain and clarify his views on these subjects, many readers today are similarly perturbed and puzzled by them. Doesn't his preference for singleness over marriage—and not just for himself but for all believers—*demean* marriage? If so, why would he oppose divorce in most cases? Do his many negative references to sexual desires reflect some deep-down anxiety about his own sexual feelings or experience? And isn't he being inconsistent when, nevertheless, he speaks of sexual intimacy as a responsibility that married partners have for each other?

Some ideas about sex and marriage that modern readers attribute to Paul derive from writings that were probably composed after his death, even though they were written in his name. For example, unlike the apostle's own letters, both Ephesians and Colossians unambiguously affirm Christian marriage by providing directions about the management of Christian households and relationships within it—including the direction that wives should be "subject" to their husbands (Eph 5:22–6:9;

Col 3:18–4:1). Marriage is also affirmed as an important Christian institution in the Pastoral Epistles (1, 2 Tim and Titus), where we also find the statement that a woman's salvation comes "through childbearing" (1 Tim 2:15). But to be fair to Paul, we must exclude these letters of questionable authorship from consideration and stick with the seven letters that he himself certainly wrote (see ch. 1). Of these, 1 Corinthians is especially important for our present topic.

Sexual Immorality

Paul's umbrella term for "sexual immorality" is *porneia*, although in some contexts this Greek word has a more specific reference. In one passage or another and in one way or another, he identifies adultery, incest, prostitution, same-sex intercourse, and giving in to uncontrolled sexual desires as contrary to the will of God, which is to say, immoral. The apostle's opposition to these practices derived primarily from his upbringing as a Jew, and probably also from the teachings of Jesus as they were remembered in the church. It is important to recognize, however, that many people outside the Jewish and Christian communities, including various moral philosophers in Paul's day, also viewed such conduct as immoral. For this reason, the apostle sometimes only *lists* such behaviors as immoral without troubling to explain why he thinks they are (Rom 1:29-31; 13:13; 1 Cor 5:10-11; 6:9-10; 2 Cor 12:20-21; Gal 5:19-21; see ch. 3 for further comments on such lists). It must also be said, however, that sexual vices constitute only a minority of the items thus cataloged. Mostly, Paul names evils like idolatry, drunkenness, quarreling, greed, arrogance, and slander. He was by no means *preoccupied* either with sex in general or with sexual vices, and we need to keep this in mind as we proceed.

Although the vice lists show us little about *why* the apostle regarded certain kinds of sexual conduct as immoral, a few other passages disclose a bit more. In Rom 13:9, quoting from his Jewish Bible (Exod 20:14; Deut 5:18), he mentions *adultery* as one of the laws summed up in the commandment to "love your neighbor as yourself" (Lev 19:18; note also Rom 2:22; 7:2-3). Along with this invoking of Scripture, Paul could also have cited Jesus' opposition to adultery (e.g., Matt 5:27-28), but he does not do so, either in Romans or elsewhere. The apostle's opposition to adultery may also be reflected in 1 Thessalonians, the earliest of his surviving letters. There, after declaring that God condemns "sexual immorality" (NRSV: "fornication"), he directs that a man should "take a wife for himself in holiness and honor" and not "wrong or exploit a brother in this matter" (4:3-6, following NRSV's alternative translations in vv. 4, 6). Given the context, the "wrong" done to a fellow believer could be adultery committed with the man's wife.

It is not surprising that Paul also opposed *incest*, which was prohibited in many ancient societies, being widely understood as including sexual relations with either blood relatives or those related by marriage. In 1 Cor 5:1-13 he directs his congregation to expel a member (vv. 2b, 5) who has been sexually intimate with his stepmother ("his father's wife"). Scriptural condemnations of such relationships could have been cited (Lev 18:8; 20:11; Deut 22:30; 27:20), but the apostle chooses instead to accentuate its wickedness by calling it "immorality . . . of a kind that is not found even among pagans" (v. 1). It is equally important to observe, however, that he criticizes not only the incestuous relationship itself but also the congregation's indifference to it (v. 2a-b).

Having sex with a prostitute is something else that the apostle regards as incompatible with belonging to Christ. His warnings on this topic, which come primarily in 1 Cor 6:12-20, have only male clients and female prostitutes in view (the prevailing type of prostitution in Greco-Roman society). Unlike the case of the incestuous man, there is no indication that any particular members of the Corinthian congregation had been involved either as prostitutes or as clients. Paul would have known, however, that prostitution was rampant in Corinth, as it certainly was in other urban centers. Roman law did not prohibit prostitution and, in fact, placed a tax on it, which endowed it with a degree of legitimacy. Prostitutes were readily available, not just in brothels but also in many public places like inns, cafés, and the baths. And many of them could be afforded even by clients of modest means. There was also, however, vigorous opposition to this commerce in sex, and not just from Jews and Christians. Various moral philosophers argued that prostitution inevitably undermines marriage and the family, thereby threatening the stability of the entire social, economic, and political order. Some also decried the exploitation of those who worked as prostitutes, the majority of whom had been recruited from the ranks of the most vulnerable and marginalized members of society—especially abandoned children, slaves and former slaves, the poor, and those of foreign birth.

Paul's argument against sexual relations with a prostitute takes a different course, however, at least as he develops it in 1 Corinthians. He makes no mention of the plight of those forced into prostitution or of the threat to marriage, family, and society in general. But neither does he oppose prostitution on the grounds that having sex is bad, for—as we shall presently see—Paul commends sex between married partners. His opposition to prostitution, which is focused not on the purveyor of sex but on the client, has a specifically theological basis. A key premise of his argument is that one's "body"—he means one's *whole self*—belongs solely to the Lord (the resurrected Christ; see 1 Cor 3:23; 6:13b-15a, 19-20). He believes that this relationship is definitive of one's true identity, and that this is violated when one buys sexual favors from a prostitute. As he sees it, in yielding to the tyranny of uncontrolled sexual desires, one has forsaken the realm where Christ is Lord and has, as it were, "deeded" oneself to the rule of malevolent powers, which is idolatry (1 Cor 6:15b-18; see also 10:6-8; Jer 5:7-8; Wis 14:12).

31

Paul's opposition to prostitution is also evident in 1 Cor 6:9 where—if the NRSV translation is correct—"male prostitutes" are listed among those said to be excluded from God's kingdom. The Greek word in question may, however, refer simply to an "effeminate" male. Or, specifically, to the male who is penetrated in same-sex intercourse—just as the following term (NRSV: "sodomites") could refer to the penetrating male, whether or not he is paying for sex. In any case, and especially when we take account of the apostle's comments in Rom 1:26-27, it would appear that he regarded *all same-sex intercourse* as immoral. Because Paul is so often cited and so variously interpreted in present-day discussions of homosexuality, this topic will receive closer attention below (ch. 3).

Finally, in accord with both Jewish Scriptures and the ancient Greek ideal of moderation in all things, Paul denounced *immoderate and uncontrolled sexual desires.* He viewed not only sexual relations with a prostitute but also adultery, incest, and same-sex intercourse as expressions of raging sexual appetites that should be restrained. The same idea underlies his charge that those "who do not know God" enter into sexual relationships out of "lustful passion" (1 Thess 4:5), and his assertion that "debauchery and licentiousness" are among the fleshly "desires" that must be put aside (Rom 13:13-14). This concern is also evident in 1 Cor 7, where he calls for the exercise of "self-control," warning that one must not be "aflame with passion" (vv. 9, 36-37). Paul did not, however, regard sexual desire as *inherently* evil. This is clear from what he says in the same passage about marriage and divorce, the two topics on which the remainder of this chapter will focus.

Marriage

The apostle's comments about marriage must be assessed with reference to the views of marriage and family that prevailed in his day, not with reference to ideas that are current today. In Roman imperial times marriage was seen not as fulfilling the emotional, sexual, or spiritual needs of the marriage partners, but as fulfilling their family, civic, and social duties. As generally conceived, the aim of marriage was to establish a household in which children could be raised who would be able to support and care for their elderly parents, to assure the continuation of the family line and traditions, and to provide for the lawful transmittal of its property to the next generation. The orderly transfer of this material and cultural legacy was regarded as vital for the welfare of society as a whole. While affection for one's spouse was sometimes commended as contributing to a stable household, a loving relationship was not regarded as the essential foundation of marriage, as it tends to be in many modern societies. This was as true for Jews as for others in the Greco-Roman world.

Under Roman law, a marriage that entailed full rights of succession and inheritance could exist only where both partners were Roman citizens or, alternatively, where they had been specifically granted the right to marry. Females were generally married between the ages of twelve and fifteen and males before the age of twenty-five. Although a period of betrothal was usual, it was not necessary. Marriages sometimes but not always involved written marriage contracts and the payment of a dowry by the bride's family. Although a marriage ceremony might have religious aspects, it was primarily a family occasion, during which the bride's father presented her to the groom before the assembled guests, who bore witness to and celebrated the formation of a new household. During the reign of Augustus (27 B.C.E.–14 C.E.), when a falling birth rate threatened to weaken the empire, laws were enacted (in 18 B.C.E. and 9 C.E.) that provided incentives for getting married and having children, and that stipulated penalties for those who remained single or childless. For the same reason, the new laws prohibited lengthy betrothals and encouraged remarriage after a divorce or the death of one's spouse.

The Corinthian Church

What we can know about Paul's view of marriage comes primarily from 1 Corinthians, written to his largely Gentile church in Corinth. At the time, Corinth was the commercially and politically important capital of the Roman province of Achaea. The ethnic, social, and economic diversity of Paul's congregation mirrored that of the city itself and contributed to the disputes about religious and moral issues that the apostle addresses in this letter. A substantial number of members apparently regarded themselves as religiously superior to their fellow believers, claiming to have been granted special knowledge about God, as well as other Spirit-bestowed gifts like speaking in tongues, prophesying, and having the power to heal (see 1 Cor 12–14). The apostle, well aware of these claims, more than once expresses concern about the religious arrogance that was threatening the spiritual health of this congregation (1 Cor 4:6, 18; 5:2; 2 Cor 12:20; compare 1 Cor 8:1; 13:4). He was also aware that the Corinthian Christians were confused about, or in some cases indifferent to, certain moral questions. We have already noted two examples: his rebuke of the Corinthians' arrogant indifference to a specific case of incest (1 Cor 5) and his equally firm but more general warning about having sex with prostitutes (1 Cor 6:12-20).

A Question from Corinth and Paul's Response

Unlike his instructions concerning incest and prostitution, Paul's counsels about marriage (1 Cor 7:1-40) are offered in response to a question addressed to him in a letter from his Corinthian church (7:1a). That question was not, however, about marriage in general, but specifically about sex. Some in the congregation may have presumed that their baptism into Christ had freed them to engage in almost any kind of sexual conduct (see 6:11b, "washed . . . sanctified . . . [and] justified in the name of the Lord Jesus Christ and in the Spirit of our God"). There seem to have been others, however, who held that sexual union either within or apart from marriage was a violation of one's belonging to Christ.

That Paul opposed the first (sometimes called libertine) view is clear from his emphatic condemnation of sex with prostitutes (note esp. 6:15-16a), which his converts had doubtless heard from him before. But now the Corinthian letter has asked him to comment on the second (sometimes called ascetic) view, that those who profess to belong to Christ must abstain from all sexual intercourse, even with a spouse. This second point of view is given in a slogan that Paul quotes (or paraphrases) in 7:1b: "It is well for a man not to touch [= have sex with] a woman." Perhaps this judgment was based on the mistaken idea that Paul intended his condemnation of sex with prostitutes to rule out *all* sexual intercourse. This is not, however, a conclusion that the apostle is willing to allow, and he goes on to make this clear in 1 Cor 7:2-6.

Paul contends that "because of cases of sexual immorality, each man should have his own wife and each woman her own husband" (v. 2). This is both a directive that marriages should be strictly monogamous and an implicit affirmation of sexual intercourse within marriage. In both respects, the apostle's Jewish heritage is evident, at least in part. According to ancient Jewish tradition, the fundamental purpose of God's creating both male and female is expressed in the divine blessing to "be fruitful and multiply" (Gen 1:28). Paul, however, does not invoke these words, either here or anywhere else. It is consistent with his sense of living at the close of history that he has nothing to say about procreation as an aim of marriage. Nor does he draw on the church's tradition, according to which Jesus had commended marriage as an institution grounded in creation itself (Mark 10:6-9, parallel Matt 19:4-6).

Paul has taken over, instead, a secondary reason for marriage, one that is found in pagan as well as Jewish sources: it is good to marry "because of sexual immoralities" (1 Cor 7:2a, my translation, which retains in English the Greek plural noun). He is commending marriage as effective in preventing untamed sexual passions from controlling a person's life, and thereby driving one into such practices as incest, prostitution, and same-sex intercourse. This claim is based on the recognition that human beings are endowed with powerful, potentially destructive sexual desires, and a belief that marriage curbs promiscuity by providing for the measured, responsible expression of those desires. A comparable viewpoint is found, for example, in the Jewish *Testament of Levi* 9:9-10 (second century B.C.E.), which advises males to "guard against promiscuity" by marrying while they are still young.

The apostle is not claiming that the *sole* or even most important reason for marrying is to damp down sexual passions. His topic is not the aims or meaning of marriage, for that is not the question the letter from Corinth had addressed to him. He is responding, rather, to the contention—which he deems to be wrong—that even within marriage sexual intercourse is a fleshly indulgence and, therefore, incompatible with being Christian.

In opposing this view, the apostle does not declare simply that sexual intimacy *is* permissible in a Christian marriage. He goes beyond that to say that sexual intimacy is a *responsibility* that each partner has toward the other: "The husband should give to his wife her conjugal rights, and likewise the wife to her husband" (1 Cor 7:3). He uses similar wording elsewhere when speaking of such obligations as paying taxes, showing respect, giving honor, and—above all—loving one another (Rom 13:7-8; also Rom 15:1, 27: being patient with those who are weak and assisting those who are poor). In the present instance, the wording suggests that he views physical sexual union as an important means by which marriage partners are to *give themselves to each other*. He is taking nothing back when, subsequently, he advises that "those who have wives" should live "as though they had none" (1 Cor 7:29). Neither this nor the following directives (vv. 29-30) call for the abandonment of everyday responsibilities, but urge believers to understand that the structures and institutions of this present age can lay no ultimate claim on their lives (v. 31).

Paul emphasizes, further, that self-giving is a *mutual* responsibility: "The wife does not have authority over her own body, but the husband does; likewise the husband does not have authority over his own body, but the wife does" (1 Cor 7:4). This view of the marriage relationship stands in stark contrast to the patriarchal conception that prevailed at the time. The Stoic philosopher Arius Didymus (first century B.C.E.–C.E.) taught that "the man has the rule of his household by nature. For the deliberative faculty of the woman is inferior, in children it does not yet exist, and in the case of slaves it is completely absent" (Stobaeus, *Anthologium*, 148-51). Although Seneca, the noted moral philosopher and statesman (died 65 C.E.), affirmed that females contribute as much to society as males do, he also said that "the one class is born to obey, the other to command" (*Moral Essays* 2, "To Selenus," 1:1). Similarly, while the historian, biographer, and essayist Plutarch (ca. 45–120 C.E.) commended certain types of sharing within a marriage (e.g., *Advice to Bride and Groom*, 143.34), he nevertheless advised husbands to exercise control over their wives, and wives to yield to the preferences of their husbands (e.g., 139.11; 142.32-33). He also specifically warned, on the one hand, that when a wife seeks to avoid or is annoyed at the sexual advances of her husband, she is being "disdainful" and "without affection" (my translation); and on the other hand, that when she tries to make sexual advances toward him, she is acting like a prostitute (*Advice to Bride and Groom*, 140.18). In the Jewish community too it was taken for granted that a marriage, including the maintenance of conjugal relations, must be entirely under the husband's direction. A rabbinic saying to this effect is typical of a long tradition: "A man is bound to please his wife with a good deed" (*Pesahim* 72b).

By contrast, Paul's statement that each partner has authority over the body of the other is a call for *mutual responsibility* that runs directly counter to the prevailing norm of male superiority and female inferiority. He leaves no room for the notion that a husband's role is to rule over his wife, while a wife's role is to yield to her husband. Moreover, there is good reason to suppose that, if asked to elaborate, he would call for mutual responsibility in all aspects of marriage. Later on in 1 Corinthians he significantly qualifies his comments about the distinctiveness of gender roles by insisting, nevertheless, on the *interdependence* of male and female: "In the Lord woman is not independent of man or man independent of woman" (1 Cor 11:11). The apostle's advocacy of this principle is consistent with his understanding of sexual intimacy as a mutual responsibility of husband and wife, and also strongly suggests that he viewed other aspects of marriage in the same way.

A commitment to the principle of mutual responsibility is further evident in Paul's comments about abstaining from conjugal relations (1 Cor 7:5-6). Here he may be thinking of celibate marriages, which seem to have been urged by some Corinthian Christians. Although he does not absolutely prohibit sexual abstinence in a marriage, he allows it only as an exception ("by way of concession, not of command"), only if it is to be temporary ("for a set time"), only if both the husband and the wife have agreed, and only if their purpose is to devote themselves fully to prayer. He believes that if spouses permanently refrain from sex with each other, one or both may be overwhelmed by sexual desires and led (by Satan) to gratify them in some form of immoral behavior. This concern underlies the apostle's frequently cited and usually misunderstood judgment that "it is better to marry than to be aflame with passion" (1 Cor 7:9b). This remark is consistent with the reason for marriage that he offered at the outset of his discussion (v. 2, "because of . . . immoralities"). It also accords with his belief that sexual intimacy between committed partners is an appropriate and even necessary constituent of their mutual self-giving, while all other sexual liaisons are driven by raw, uncontrolled passions. His intention is not to demean marriage, but to commend it as a relationship in which otherwise destructive and shameful sexual desires find constructive and honorable expression.

Paul's Own Preference

Given his endorsement of marriage and sexual intimacy within it, why does the apostle nevertheless hold that it is better to be single, as he himself is (1 Cor 7:7)? There is, indeed, no evidence that he ever had a wife. His preference surfaces several more times as he responds to the letter from Corinth. In his opinion, Christians who have never married should remain single (1 Cor 7:8, 25-26, 27c-d), those who are betrothed should not proceed to marriage (vv. 37, 38b), those who are left single by the death of a spouse should not remarry (vv. 8, 40a; compare v. 27c-d), and those who are divorced should not remarry, unless to the former spouse (v. 11; compare vv. 25-26). Although some interpreters summarily dismiss these counsels as biased, ill conceived, or simply eccentric, a closer reading of Paul's discussion will show them to be generally well thought out and consistent.

It is important to observe, first of all, that *Paul's preference for singleness is formed strictly on the basis of practical, not moral, considerations.* Nowhere does he say or imply that marriage is wrong, and more than once he emphasizes that it is *not* a "sin" to marry (1 Cor 7:28, 36). For him, it is not being married that is morally problematic but being single, because he believes that, in general, singles are driven into immoral conduct by their sexual desires (7:2, 9b; also vv. 36-37).

Paul's actual reason for preferring the single state is his wish to spare believers the "distress in this life" that he assumes they will have if they marry (1 Cor 7:28). He appears to be thinking of the anxieties that a husband and wife experience as they apply themselves to the many tasks involved in supporting each other, rearing children, and maintaining a household (vv. 32-35). He warns that these everyday concerns will detract from their ability to "please the Lord" (v. 32; compare v. 34, commitment to "the affairs of the Lord," and v. 35, "unhindered devotion to the Lord"). In the context of this passage and the letter overall, devotion to the Lord includes a resolve to be "holy in body and spirit" (v. 34b), to lead a well-ordered life (v. 35), and to contribute to the well-being ("salvation") of others (10:32-33)—the latter being emphasized in various ways and connections (e.g., 10:24; 12:7, 20-26; 13:1-13; 14:1-5; 16:14).

Second, *Paul takes it for granted that entering into a marriage necessarily and properly requires committing oneself to the well-being of one's spouse.* This consequential assumption underlies his whole discussion in 1 Cor 7. Although he is glad that he himself is not encumbered with the anxieties that husbands and wives typically experience, he neither denies the importance of the responsibilities that produce those anxieties nor reproaches believers for carrying them out. Indeed, we may reasonably infer that if his intention had been (like Plutarch's, noted above) to offer advice to a bride and groom, he would have stressed the importance of their fulfilling the marital, parental, and household obligations they had undertaken. Paul's statement that "the married man is anxious about the affairs of the world, how to please his wife" and "the married woman is anxious about the affairs of the world, how to please her husband" (vv. 33-34) is not an indictment of marriage but a simple assertion of fact. Moreover, his use of identical phrasing in the two parts of this statement is further evidence that he views marriage as a partnership in which obligations run both ways.

Third, *Paul's preference for singleness does not lead him to say that all believers should remain single or even that they should try to remain single.* His preference is hardly stated before he significantly qualifies it. Yes, it is better for believers to be single than married—"but each has a particular gift [Greek: *charisma*] from God, one having one kind and another a different kind" (7:7b). This qualification is in line with his contention that God has apportioned diverse spiritual gifts (*charismata*) to those who belong to Christ; there is no "standard bundle" of gifts that comes with baptism. For example, not all believers have been given the ability to prophesy, to speak ecstatically ("in tongues"), or to interpret ecstatic utterances (1 Cor 12:4-11). Accordingly, in the present instance Paul's qualifying sentence amounts to an acknowledgment that he can remain single only because he has a "particular" gift that other unmarried folk may not have. He means, apparently, the gift of moral strength to repress, or at least rise above, the otherwise uncontrollable sexual desires to which, he believes, a single person is especially vulnerable.

Finally, *when Paul has occasion to speak of Christians who happen to be married, there is not the slightest hint that he regards their married status as compromising their commitment to the Lord or their labors on the Lord's behalf.* This very letter (1 Cor) offers three telling examples:

(1) When he points out that "the other apostles and the brothers of the Lord and Cephas [Peter]" all have wives (9:5), Paul's intention is not to criticize them for being married but to claim the same right for himself (even though he has not exercised it).

(2) He expresses high regard for Stephanas, the head of the first household converted in Corinth and now a leader in the Corinthian church (1:16; 16:15-18). Stephanas and the other members of this household are commended as being "devoted . . . to the service of the saints [other believers]" and deserving of the church's support. Paul requests, in addition, that the congregation "give recognition" to people like the three emissaries—including Stephanas—who have recently come to him as its representatives.

(3) Paul extends greetings from the married couple Aquila and Prisca and the church that meets in their house (16:19). The author of Acts (who identifies the wife as "Priscilla") portrays them as former residents of Corinth and close associates of Paul (Acts 18:2, 18, 26). The apostle himself says not only that they work side by side with him "in Christ Jesus" but also that they have "risked their necks" for his life (Rom 16:3-4).

In sum, although Paul sees certain practical advantages in being single, he neither demeans marriage nor claims that being married prevents sincere devotion to the Lord. In fact, he knows and names married believers who have served the gospel in extraordinary and exemplary ways.

Divorce

Under Roman laws in effect at the time of Paul, it was as easy to dissolve a marriage as to form one in the first place. Divorce could be initiated by either spouse and for almost any reason. Adultery, however, was the most usual cause, and wives were more often charged with it than husbands. Where a woman's husband or father presented evidence of her adultery that was deemed compelling, the husband was required to divorce his wife at once. Within the Jewish community, however, divorce was less common, perhaps because the union of male and female was regarded as divinely ordained, an integral part of God's creation (Gen 1:27-28; 2:18-25). Nonetheless, divorce was an option—albeit only for husbands, who could take such action for a wide variety of reasons (e.g., Deut 24:1-4).

Traditions contained in the Synoptic Gospels suggest that Jesus took a much stricter stand against divorce than most Jewish teachers of his day. According to the version of his teaching in Matt 5:31-32, he specifically opposed the provision for divorce found in Deut 24:1-4, declaring that any husband who divorces his wife causes her to commit adultery. The only exception that Jesus allowed, according to Matthew, was in the case of a wife's infidelity (Matt 5:31-32; 19:1-12; in both places NRSV translates *porneia* as "unchastity"). According to Mark 10:1-12 (which, in line with Roman law, assumes that either spouse has the right to divorce), Jesus allowed for no exceptions at all (compare Luke 16:18). While both Matthew and Mark portray Jesus as speaking of marriage as established with creation itself, in Mark's account (generally regarded as an earlier form of the tradition) Jesus also declares that the law's provision for divorce (Deut 24) is a concession to human weakness ("hardness of heart," Mark 10:5).

Paul's Advice for Christian Couples

Despite Paul's preference for singleness, he directs that Christians who are already married at the time of their conversion should be governed by Jesus' prohibition of divorce: "To the married I give this command—not I but the Lord—that the wife should not separate from her husband . . . and that the husband should not divorce his wife" (1 Cor 7:10, 11b; in vv. 10-11 "separate" and "divorce" are used interchangeably). Like the author of the gospel of Mark, who wrote some twenty years later, the apostle presumes that either a husband or a wife can opt for divorce, but also that Jesus' prohibition of divorce was absolute and unqualified. The apostle does not just quote Jesus and let it go at that, however. We do not see him imposing a commandment that must be obeyed, no matter what. We see him taking account of the fact that the situation in one marriage may differ from that in another.

Paul's attentiveness to varying circumstances is already apparent when he says, parenthetically, that "if [a woman] does separate," she should either "remain unmarried" or "be reconciled to her husband" (7:11a). Although he does not restate this principle when speaking of a man who divorces his wife (v. 11b), he probably intends for it to be applied in that case as well. However reluctantly, he recognizes that there are, indeed, bound to be instances in which divorce will occur despite the Lord's commandment.

It is not surprising that Paul favors the couple's reconciliation when it is possible; and the advice that otherwise the woman (or man) should "remain unmarried" is consistent with his stated preference for singleness. One wonders, however, why he makes no specific provision for the possibility that the woman (or man) may lack the "gift" to remain single. Perhaps he intends his immediately preceding comment about "the unmarried and the widows" to apply here as well—"if they are not practicing self-control, they should marry" (7:9). About one important matter, however, there is no question: despite his principled opposition to divorce, Paul does not presume to stand in judgment over either of the parties involved, nor does he instruct the congregation to discipline them in any way.

What If the Spouse Is an Unbeliever?

The counsels about divorce in 1 Cor 7:10-11 concern marriages in which both partners are Christian. Probably in most cases, the conversion of the male head of a household meant also the conversion of his wife (Plutarch advised that a woman should worship "only the gods that her husband believes in" [*Advice to Bride and Groom*, 140.19]) and everyone else who belonged to that household, including children, extended family, and slaves (e.g., the household of Stephanas, 1 Cor 1:16; 16:15). Nonetheless, in Corinth and elsewhere there were instances in which a husband (or a wife) had been converted and the spouse remained an unbeliever. Paul addresses this situation in 1 Cor 7:12-16. Should the converted partner remain in such a marriage, or should the marriage be dissolved?

We (and the Corinthians) might suppose that Paul's condemnation of sex with prostitutes as incompatible with belonging to Christ (1 Cor 6:12-20) would also rule out marriage to an unbeliever. The apostle does, indeed, direct that a believer should not *form* a marriage with an unbeliever (Christian widows who remarry are to do so "only in the Lord," 7:39). But against our expectation, he advises that the converted partner in an *existing* marriage should, if possible, remain in that relationship (vv. 12-13). He identifies this as his own command, not the Lord's, thereby taking responsibility for applying Jesus' directive to a situation for which it had not been specifically formulated.

The apostle's primary reason for this extension of Jesus' prohibition of divorce is that even "mixed" marriages can be affirmed as *holy* (7:14a). This is a clear rejection of any notion of such marriages as "unclean" merely because one partner is an unbeliever. Quite the contrary, Paul maintains that the unbeliever is "made holy" through the believing spouse. Interpreters differ on how "made holy" is to be understood here. Paul certainly does not mean that the unbelieving spouse is "saved," because he will go on to mention conversion only as a possibility (v. 16). He most likely means that the unbeliever is drawn into the sphere of God's holiness as it is manifested in the life of the Christian partner— who, like all believers, has been "sanctified [made holy] in Christ Jesus" and called to be among the "saints [holy ones]" (1:2). Otherwise, Paul argues, the couple's children could not be holy, as he believes (for whatever reason) they are (7:14b).

But what if the unbelieving spouse wants to divorce? In this case, Paul says, the believer should "let it be so" (7:15a), for he or she "is not bound" to maintain such a marriage (v. 15b). Although the apostle has directed that a believer who opts for divorce should remain unmarried (or be reconciled to the original spouse, v. 11a), he would apparently place no such restriction on a believer who has been divorced by an unbelieving spouse.

Still addressing the situation faced by believers who are married to unbelievers, Paul declares, "It is to peace that God has called you" (7:15c). Is this to be read with verse 15b as a reason for accepting the divorce instigated by an unbelieving spouse (divorce is better than a marriage fraught with discord)? Or is it to be read with verses 12-14 as another reason to *remain* in a mixed marriage (thus avoiding the disruption and pain that attend the breakup of a marriage)? It is possible that Paul intends it to be read in both ways.

In concluding his counsels about mixed marriages, the apostle holds out the possibility that the unbelieving partner might eventually be won over to the gospel (7:16; here "save" means "convert"). It is not clear whether he thinks there is a reasonably good or only a slim chance of the unbeliever's conversion. In either case, the comment reinforces his advice that a believer should not divorce an unbelieving spouse who is willing to remain in the marriage. We should also note, however, that Paul does not direct or even encourage the believing spouse to try to convert the unbeliever; he regards and addresses the believing partners in such marriages as wives and husbands, not as evangelists.

Observations and Reflections

In assessing Paul's thought, we have to take account of the imposing divide that separates the social, political, and cultural realities and institutions of the first century from those of the twenty-first. We must also acknowledge that Paul was wrong in believing that the "end" of human history and the promised salvation would occur during his lifetime (e.g., 1 Cor 7:31b; 15:12-28). Even though we know that life on our planet is at risk in various ways and for various reasons, this knowledge is still a far cry from Paul's belief in the imminence of the Lord's return and the coming of the kingdom. Our modern understanding of the world and history does not require us to dismiss summarily Paul's counsels about sex, marriage, and divorce. It does require us, however, to be mindful of the differences between his worldview and ours, as well as of differences between the circumstances with which he had to reckon and those we face today. Accordingly, we must not lose sight of the historical and cultural distance that separates us from Paul's world, even as we consider how his thought may, nonetheless, still challenge and enrich our own.

1. *Paul's letters provide us with no generalized, comprehensive statement of his views about sex, marriage, and divorce.* His most extensive counsels about these topics occur in 1 Corinthians, a letter that he wrote in response to the particular needs and concerns of his Corinthian congregation. As a result, we know nothing about his views on a number of the issues commonly discussed by his contemporaries (like the Hellenistic moral philosophers and Jewish teachers of the law) when they address this same trio of topics.

The apostle's silence about the overall aims of marriage is not surprising, given his firm belief that the end time was near. For instance, most of Paul's contemporaries (both Jewish and non-Jewish) regarded the bearing and rearing of children as the most important function of marriage. But for Paul to have *encouraged* childbearing would have been in tension with his end-time expectation (and thus, his preference for singleness); and for him to have *discouraged* childbearing would have been in tension with his opposition to sexual abstinence within a marriage.

Yet he also said nothing, one way or the other, about the rearing of children (e.g., their status in case the parents divorce), household management, spousal abuse, child abuse, premarital sex, contraception, or abortion. Although we might *infer* what he would say about some or all of these, the fact remains that he did not specifically address any of them. We do not know whether he was or was not indifferent to such matters; we know only that he seems to have had no occasion to comment on them in the letters that have come down to us.

2. Because Paul recognized that individual situations and circumstances vary, his counsels about sex, marriage, and divorce in 1 Cor 7 are not stated as moral absolutes. To be sure, because—rightly or wrongly—he viewed all extramarital sex as evidence of uncontrolled sexual passions, his condemnation of adultery, incest, prostitution, and same-sex intercourse was unqualified by circumstantial considerations. But in commenting on other matters he often employed expressions that designated an action as simply advantageous or good or "better" than another (vv. 1b, 8, 9, 26b, 37, 38), thereby stopping short of identifying it as the *absolutely best* or *only permissible* one. Thus, for example, while he affirmed singleness as *relatively better* than marriage, he did not view it as *absolutely good,* for he also identified instances where marriage was relatively better than singleness. Similarly, while he believed that maintaining a marriage was *relatively better* than ending it through divorce, he noted that sometimes ending a marriage through divorce was *relatively better* than maintaining it.

Moreover, we have seen that Paul generally recognized that circumstances can vary substantially from one situation to another, and along with them the specific moral issues and options with which one must grapple. His concern to take individual circumstances into account can be quite objectively documented simply by listing the numerous conditional clauses that occur in his discussion of marriage and divorce (1 Cor 7), each of which identifies a real or possible situation that calls for special consideration:

> But if they are not practicing self-control. . . . (v. 9)
> But if she does separate. . . . (v. 11a)
> If any believer has a wife who is an unbeliever. . . . (v. 12)
> If any woman has a husband who is an unbeliever. . . . (v. 13)
> But if the unbelieving partner separates. . . . (v. 15)

> But if you marry. . . . (v. 28)
>
> If a virgin marries. . . . (v. 28)
>
> If anyone thinks. . . . (v. 36)
>
> If his passions are strong. . . . (v. 36)
>
> But if the husband dies. . . . (v. 39)

One especially noteworthy variable that Paul took into account was the particular divine "gift(s)" with which a believer is endowed. As we have seen, he acknowledged that the gift that enables a person to remain single is not bestowed on everyone. Whether he also thought that people who lack that gift have, instead, *a gift for marriage* is unclear. It is entirely clear, however, that he neither flaunted his gift for singleness as superior to others nor demeaned those who did not have it. Later in 1 Corinthians he emphasized that the "varieties of gifts" that are manifested in the believing community all come from the "same Spirit," the "same Lord," and the "same God," and are to be used for the benefit of all (12:4-7). In his view, therefore, no gift represents an achievement of the one who has it, no gift is inherently better than any other, and every gift is intended to equip the recipient for contributing to the well-being of others (the latter being true even of ecstatic utterance, when it is interpreted). He therefore urged believers to consider what is morally right and possible *given their own individual situations* and then to apply themselves to fulfilling that good.

3. *Paul's comments about marriage pertain not just to the question of its compatibility with life in Christ, but also to the character and quality of the marital relationship.* In his earliest surviving letter the apostle advised his Thessalonian converts that a man should "know how to take a wife for himself in holiness and honor, not with lustful passion, like the Gentiles who do not know God" (1 Thess 4:4-5 NRSV alternative translation). This advice corresponds to the narrative of Tobias's marriage to Sarah as presented in a writing that was part of the Greek version of Scripture used

49

by Paul. On their wedding night, Tobias takes note of God's creation of Eve to be Adam's "helper and support" and then expresses his commitment to Sarah. After vowing that he takes her as his wife "not because of lust, / but with sincerity," he prays that God will bless their marriage: "Grant that she and I may find mercy / and that we may grow old together" (Tob 8:6-7). Paul's advice to the Thessalonians situates him in the tradition represented by this story. With the blessing of God, a man and a woman are joined together in marriage as lifelong companions. When a marriage is formed with this commitment, it demonstrates the "holiness" and "honor" to which the apostle refers.

Paul's counsels about marriage in 1 Corinthians continue to reflect this same point of view. We have seen that he allowed no exception to the principle that a man should have but one wife and that a woman should have but one husband (7:2). We have observed, as well, that he viewed marriage as properly a partnership that requires mutual trust and respect and the sharing of decisions and responsibilities (7:3-4, 5-6, 33-34; compare 11:11). And not least, we have noted his belief that a Christian household should be a place of holiness (7:14) and peace (7:15c).

Although he had nothing to say about sexual fulfillment or pleasure as an appropriate end of marriage, he regarded sexual intimacy between a husband and a wife as important for their well-being, both as individuals and as a couple. This set him apart from some Corinthian Christians who held that one's belonging to Christ ruled out sexual intercourse. It also set him apart from certain moral philosophers who argued that having sex within a marriage should serve only the purpose of begetting children. For Paul, what legitimated marriage was not the biblical mandate to "be fruitful and multiply," and certainly not the imperial call for larger families, it was the need of two people for each other, provided they are willing to commit themselves to each other in a mutually faithful and caring relationship.

4. Paul conveyed his views as authoritative counsels, yet he neither repre-sented them as commands nor supposed that they relieved his congregation of the task of moral discernment in particular cases. What we find in chapter 7 of 1 Corinthians is not a list of arbitrary rules but an exemplary instance of the apostle's own *moral reasoning.* When responding to the request for advice from the Corinthian church, he sought to *instruct* and *persuade,* not to bully it into complying with some preformulated "code of sexual ethics."

There is no doubt that Paul, like the prophets of ancient Israel, under-stood himself as divinely commissioned to proclaim the word of God (e.g., Gal 1:11-17; 1 Thess 2:4). His sense of apostolic authority is evident throughout 1 Corinthians, and so is his expectation that the letter's recip-ients will acknowledge that authority (e.g., 1 Cor 1:1, 10; 9:16-17; 14:37; 15:8-11). He encouraged the Corinthian believers to think of him as their "father" and to be guided by his "ways in Christ Jesus" (4:14-17). In particular, he wanted them to receive his advice about sex, marriage, and divorce as the judgment of "one who by the Lord's mercy is trustworthy" and has "the Spirit of God" (7:25, 40).

At the same time, however, Paul was reserved in the use of this author-ity, not wanting to "lord it over" the faith of his converts (2 Cor 1:24). In 1 Cor 7 this reticence is apparent when he takes care to say that the "command" against divorce is not his own but the Lord's (v. 10), and again when he points out that his application of that command to mixed marriages is his own doing, not the Lord's (v. 12). Similarly, he cautions the Corinthians to interpret his permission for temporary abstention from marital sex as a "concession," not as a "command" (v. 6), and he says that his advice about remaining single is not intended "to put any restraint upon [them], but to promote good order and unhindered devotion to the Lord" (v. 35).

Earlier in 1 Corinthians Paul had asked rhetorically whether his congregation would prefer him to come to them next time "with a stick, or with love in a spirit of gentleness" (4:21). Although the question identifies the "stick" as a clear option, there is no doubt that the apostle preferred to exercise his apostolic authority "with love in a spirit of gentleness." He had said as much in an earlier letter written (from Corinth) to the church in Thessalonica: although he and his fellow missionaries "might have made demands as apostles of Christ," they chose, rather, to deal with the new converts "like a nurse tenderly caring for her own children" (1 Thess 2:7). This, in fact, is how Paul responded to the Corinthians' questions about sex, marriage, and divorce. He was authoritative but not authoritarian in presenting his views. And he took account of special circumstances, allowing that the moral issues and options were apt to vary from one situation to another.

For Further Reading

Ancient sources cited in this chapter: the *Testament of Levi* is cited from the translation in James H. Charlesworth, ed., *The Old Testament Pseudepigrapha* (2 vols.; Garden City, N.Y.: Doubleday, 1983); the saying from the *Pesahim* is cited from the translation in Isadore Epstein, ed., *The Babylonian Talmud* (London: Soncino, 1935–1959); the comment by Arius Didymus that is found in J. Stobaeus (*Anthologium*, 148-51) is cited according to the translation in M. Eugene Boring, Klaus Berger, and Carsten Colpe, *Hellenistic Commentary to the New Testament* (Nashville: Abingdon Press, 1995), #890, 530; Seneca and Plutarch are cited, except as noted, from the translations in the Loeb Classical Library (Cambridge, Mass.: Harvard University Press, various years).

Further sources and discussions pertinent to sex, marriage, and divorce in the Greco-Roman world: Judith Evans Grubbs, *Women and the Law in* the Roman Empire: A Sourcebook on Marriage, Divorce and Widowhood (London and New York: Routledge, 2002); Beryl Rawson, ed., *Marriage, Divorce, and Children in Ancient Rome* (Canberra: Humanities Research Center; Oxford: Clarendon; New York: Oxford University Press, 1991); Shaye J. D. Cohen, *The Jewish Family in Antiquity* (Brown Judaic Studies 289; Atlanta: Scholars Press, 1993); and J. Paul Sampley, ed., *Paul in the Greco-Roman World: A Handbook* (Harrisburg, Penn.: Trinity Press International, 2003)—see especially the essays by James C. Walters (adoption and inheritance), 42–76; David L. Balch (families and households), 258–92; O. Larry Yarbrough (marriage and divorce), 404–28; L. Michael White (the *pater familias*), 457–87.

See also the following volumes in the series Family, Religion, and Culture: Leo G. Perdue, ed., *Families in Ancient Israel* (Louisville: Westminster John Knox, 1997); Carolyn Osiek and David L. Balch, *Families in the New Testament World: Households and House Churches* (Louisville: Westminster John Knox, 1997); Herbert Anderson et al., eds., *The Family Handbook* (Louisville: Westminster John Knox, 1998)— see especially the essays by Tikva Frymer-Kensky (ancient Israel), 277–81; S. Scott Bartchy (the Greco-Roman world), 282–86; Margaret M. Mitchell (1 Cor 7), 249–53; Carolyn Osiek (early Christianity), 287–90.

Paul's views of sex, marriage, and divorce are discussed in several essays included in the volume by Dale B. Martin, *Sex and the Single Savior: Gender and Sexuality in Biblical Interpretation* (Louisville: Westminster John Knox, 2006).

Commentaries on 1 Corinthians: Richard B. Hays, *First Corinthians* (Interpretation; Louisville: John Knox, 1997); Richard A. Horsley, *1 Corinthians* (Abingdon New Testament Commentaries; Nashville: Abingdon Press, 1998); David John Lull, *1 Corinthians* (Chalice Commentaries for Today; St. Louis, Mo.: Chalice Press, 2007); J. Paul

Sampley, "The First Letter to the Corinthians," in *The New Interpreter's Bible* 10 (Nashville: Abingdon Press, 2002), 771–1003. More detailed: Raymond F. Collins, *First Corinthians* (Sacra Pagina; Collegeville, Minn.: Liturgical Press, 1999); Gordon D. Fee, *The First Epistle to the Corinthians* (New International Commentary on the New Testament; Grand Rapids: Eerdmans, 1987).

CHAPTER 3

HOMOSEXUALITY?

W hen a group of representative laypersons and clergy in a major Protestant denomination was asked to indicate the sources that had contributed to their "present attitudes and opinions concerning homosexuality," Scripture was named significantly more often than any other source as having contributed the most. The same poll disclosed that a high percentage of those questioned believed that "homosexual activity is a sin." As it happens, several of the scriptural passages that people cite as the most definitive for this topic are found in the letters of Paul. We have already taken account of places in which the apostle identifies adultery, incest, prostitution, and immoderate or uncontrolled sexual desires as forms of sexual immorality (ch. 2). Now we must ask what he had to say about homosexuality.

Immediately, however, we face a serious difficulty. The question mark I have placed after the title of this chapter is intended to signal what is actually a twofold difficulty. There was no word for *homosexuality* in any ancient language, including the biblical languages (Hebrew, Aramaic, Greek); nor were there any words for *heterosexuality* or *bisexuality*. Both the physical and the behavioral aspects of sex were matters of observation and discussion. But the ancient world had no conception of *sexuality* as it is commonly understood today, as a "person's sexual identity in relation to the gender to which he or she is typically attracted; the fact of being heterosexual, homosexual, or bisexual; sexual orientation" (*Oxford English Dictionary*).

To be sure, there were various ancient attempts to account for the fact that some people are erotically attracted to persons of their own sex. According to the myth famously recounted by Aristophanes in Plato's *Symposium*, 189-93 (fifth century B.C.E.), there were originally three sexes: man, woman, and a combination of the two, each of these three having two faces, four hands, four feet, and so on. But when these human beings attacked the gods, Zeus punished them by cutting each in two, so each ended up severed from its other half. From that time on, as the myth relates it, each half has wandered the earth looking for the other half: the man-woman, now two, desiring to be reunited with the opposite sex; the woman, now two, desiring to be reunited with her female half; and the man, now two, desiring to be reunited with his male half.

There were also other "explanations" of sexual attraction, including two theories advanced in the second century C.E. Ptolemy, the famous Egyptian astronomer and astrologer, believed that the nature of a person's sexual desires is determined by the constellation under which she or he is born. And Soranus, a Greek physician, regarded sexual desire for a person of the same sex as a disease of the mind. These theories, like Plato's myth, are clear evidence that ancient cultures were interested in accounting for same-sex attraction. But no ancient account of sexual attraction comes close to the understanding of sexual identity and orientation that has been gained in the last hundred years or so, through painstaking biological, psychological, and sociological research. Moreover, it is significant that no biblical writer or tradition shows any awareness of these ancient myths and speculations. The biblical accounts of creation, for instance, take no account of same-sex attraction, presuming that sexual attraction occurs only between males and females (see below).

Strictly speaking, then, there is nothing in the Bible, including the letters of Paul, about homosexuality. This concept emerged only in the second half of the nineteenth century with the advent of modern medical and psychological research into human sexuality. The word *homosexual* seems to have been coined first in German by a Hungarian-German physician, Károly M. [Kertbeny] Benkert. He used it in a private letter (to Karl Heinrich Ulrichs, May 6, 1868), and later in pamphlets, with reference to "male or female individuals" who "from birth" are erotically oriented toward their own sex. The use of the word in English is attested only from the last decade of the nineteenth century, and as we shall see, it made its first appearance in an English Bible only in 1946. When the words *homosexual* and *homosexuality* are used in this chapter in reference to ancient sources, one should always think of them as enclosed in quotation marks. In general, it is better to speak of same-sex or homoerotic relationships and the like.

Our first steps on the way to understanding what Paul says on this topic will be to consider, in turn, how same-sex activity was viewed in the Jewish Scriptures known to the apostle, and by the ancient Mediterranean world in general.

Paul's Bible

Even after his call to apostleship, Paul's faith and thought continued to be shaped by the Jewish Scriptures, although he read them now from the standpoint of his new life in Christ. All of his scriptural citations are to the Bible that was shared by Jews and Christians of his day—which the church first started calling the Old Testament only many decades after Paul's death. He ordinarily cited it according to the Septuagint (abbreviated LXX), which was a Greek version of the Hebrew Bible.

As we turn to a consideration of several Old Testament passages that have loomed large in modern discussions of homosexuality, we need to keep two important points in mind. First, same-sex activity is not a prominent topic in any of the biblical writings or in the traditions that they incorporate. There are only a few scattered passages where same-sex relationships are mentioned or portrayed. Second, Paul never specifically calls on these texts for what they say or imply about same-sex activity. He certainly knew them, however, and they may have helped inform his thinking on this matter. We shall consider, first, a story about Sodom; second, a rule in the book of Leviticus; and third, the Genesis creation accounts.

The Men of Sodom: Genesis 19:1-25

The ancient tale of Abraham's nephew, Lot, and the men of Sodom has been cited for centuries as proof that homosexuality is contrary to the will of God. In English, terms derived from the name of the city have been used at least since the end of the thirteenth century to designate (male) same-sex activity (sodomy) and those who engage in it (sodomites). However, in every instance where the word *sodomite* was used in the King James Version (1611), the Hebrew expression is properly translated as "male cult prostitute," as it is in almost all modern versions. In fact, no word for sodomite appears in the Hebrew Bible, and in the Septuagint Sodomite appears only in Gen 19:4, where it refers to male residents of Sodom.

The overall plot of the story about the men of Sodom is readily summarized. One evening, Lot (himself an "alien" in Sodom, v. 9) comes across two strangers who seem to have nowhere to spend the night. In accord with ancient customs concerning hospitality to strangers, Lot offers them lodging in his home (vv. 1-3). He does not know that they are actually angels—extraterrestrial beings!—in disguise (vv. 1, 15). When some men of the city surround Lot's house because they want to have sex with these guests, Lot offers them his virgin daughters instead (vv. 4-8). Here we see ancient expectations concerning hospitality to strangers and the protection of male honor taking precedence over even a father's protection of his daughters. When the ruffians decline Lot's offer and threaten to break down the door, the angels—being angels—strike them with blindness, thereby keeping themselves and their host from harm (vv. 9-11). The subsequent destruction of Sodom and neighboring Gomorrah is interpreted thereafter as God's judgment against the evil designs of Lot's neighbors (vv. 12-25).

This is not a story about homosexual behavior in general, and certainly not a story about homosexual acts performed by consenting adults in a committed, loving relationship. It is a story about hospitality, male honor, and violent intent—which, had it been carried out, would have been in this case same-sex rape. Eventually, Sodom did come to stand for homosexuality in general, hence the coining of the words *sodomy* and *sodomites*. But in the Bible itself, Sodom stands for evil of various kinds, and for the judgment that God will visit upon all who continue in it. One notes, for example, that the "abominable things" specifically attributed to Sodom in Ezek 16:49-50 are pride, gluttony, excessive prosperity, and indifference to those in need: "This was the guilt of your sister Sodom: she and her daughters had pride, excess of food, and prosperous ease, but did not aid the poor and needy. They were haughty, and did abominable things before me; therefore I removed them when I saw it."

A Levitical Rule: Leviticus 18:22 and 20:13

The only direct prohibition of same-sex intercourse anywhere in the Bible, Old Testament or New Testament, is a rule that occurs in two different formulations in Leviticus: "You shall not lie with a male as with a woman; it is an abomination" (18:22); and "If a man lies with a male as

59

with a woman, both of them have committed an abomination; they shall be put to death; their blood is upon them" (20:13). This rule occurs in a section of Leviticus (chs. 17–26) known to scholars as the Holiness Code, a compilation of various kinds of laws, which, in its present form, is usually dated to the sixth century B.C.E. The underlying aim of this legislation, most of it addressed to adult males, was to ensure the distinctiveness and integrity of Israel as the chosen people of the one true God.

Situated between sections that are addressed, respectively, to both the priests and the people of Israel (17:2) and to just the priests (21:1), chapters 18–20 are addressed to just the people (18:2). The importance of the extended family in ancient Israel accounts for the inclusion in this section of a number of laws intended to preserve the family's integrity by prohibiting incestuous relationships (18:7-16). Following on these, there are prohibitions that forbid relationships considered to be "unclean" and "defiling": there shall be no intercourse with a menstruating woman or with the wife of a blood relative; there shall be no offering of a child in sacrifice to a foreign god; there shall be no intercourse with another male; and there shall be no intercourse with an animal (18:19-23). In chapter 19, the legislation is somewhat miscellaneous, ranging from instructions about sacrifices and harvesting to appeals concerning just actions and loving the neighbor. Here we find, as well, rules against crossbreeding cattle, sowing two kinds of seed in one field, wearing two kinds of fabric, eating meat with blood in it, and so on. The legislation in chapter 20 is probably later than and based upon the laws in chapters 18 and 19. Here again there is a list that identifies prohibited sexual relationships (vv. 10-16), including male same-sex intercourse (v. 13); but now the death penalty is specified for these and some other offenses (vv. 1-9), presumably because they were considered to be especially grave.

There is no question that the Levitical rule in 18:22 and 20:13 explicitly and unequivocally condemns male same-sex intercourse. We must ask, however, *why* this was regarded as such a serious offense and so unconditionally condemned. Light is shed on this question when we take into consideration the overall aim of the Holiness Code and several details about the rule.

1. The most fundamental summons of this code is to *holiness*, and this summons, like holiness itself, has a theological basis: "Speak to all the congregation of the people of Israel and say to them: You shall be holy, for I the LORD your God am holy" (19:2; see also 20:7-8). To be holy means to be set apart for the service of the holy God; and to be set apart *for* the service of God requires being set apart *from* all foreign gods and the ungodly ways of those who worship them: "You shall be holy to me; for I the LORD am holy, and I have separated you from the other peoples to be mine" (20:26).

Accordingly, the intent of the rules in Lev 17–26 is to identify what is required and what is prohibited if Israel is to remain faithful to its calling as God's holy people. We may think of these rules as boundary markers designed to separate Israel from its godless neighbors: "You shall not do as they do in the land of Egypt, where you lived, and you shall not do as they do in the land of Canaan, to which I am bringing you. You shall not follow their statutes" (18:3). To help secure these boundaries, the code calls on Israel to obey the commandments that bring life (e.g., 18:4-5)—for example, the commandments to honor one's parents (19:3), provide for those who are poor (19:9-10), be just in dealing with others (19:11, 13-16), and love one's neighbor (19:18). But most especially, the code prohibits actions that were regarded as polluting and defiling because they involve the mingling or mixing of *kinds* that God, from the beginning, ordained to be separate. The rules against having incestuous relationships, sowing two kinds of seed in a field, wearing two kinds of fabrics, and engaging in male same-sex intercourse are all prohibitions of this sort. Hence the warning, "Do not defile yourselves in any of these ways, for by all these practices the nations I am casting out before you have defiled themselves" (18:24). In these and numerous other instances, the concern is not about *moral* impurity but *ritual* impurity—defilement in a physical sense. The rule about same-sex intercourse demonstrates this very well.

2. In both versions of this rule, male same-sex intercourse is identified as an "abomination" (18:22; 20:13). Here and elsewhere, the Hebrew word is used of actions that are "taboo," which is to say, totally unacceptable within the Israelite community. As Phyllis Bird has indicated,

> [*Abomination*] is not an ethical term, but a term of boundary marking. In its basic sense of taboo it describes a feeling of abhorrence and revulsion that requires or admits no rational explanation. . . . It belongs to the language of separation and distinctness from the nations that came to expression during the exile and was applied retroactively to earlier stages of Israelite history.

In other words, when something is called an abomination, that does not represent the end result of a process of moral reasoning. It is, rather, an expression of revulsion rooted in long-standing cultural conventions and habits of thought. How this works in the case of the rule about same-sex intercourse is evident in two ways.

First, neither version of the rule reflects or allows for any sort of moral reasoning. No consideration is given to what the circumstances or character of a male same-sex relationship might be. Is it consensual? Has one party, perhaps an adult male, forced himself on the other, perhaps a boy? Has one party purchased the sexual favors of the other? Nor is consideration given to whether the relationship is good or just or loving. And since no account is taken of particular circumstances, the parties involved are assumed to be equally at fault; even if one has been victimized by the other, the rule decrees that *both* have committed an "abomination" and that *both* deserve to die (20:13).

Second, the rule refers to the prohibited act as a man lying "with a male as with a woman." This phrasing shows the patriarchal orientation of the prohibition and why specifically *male* same-sex intercourse is so unconditionally condemned. From the point of view of the Holiness Code, male same-sex intercourse violates the honor of both partners; the penetrated male dishonors himself by submitting as only a female should submit, and the penetrating male dishonors himself by dominating another male. Both are departing from the culturally defined expectations concerning the distinctive sexual roles of men and women.

The Creation Accounts: Genesis 1:1–2:4a and 2:4b-24

The creation accounts of Gen 1–2 are often invoked in discussions of marriage and sexuality, including homosexuality. The account in 2:4b-24 is the earlier of the two and derives from the Yahwistic tradition (so named because its usual designation of God is Yahweh), while the account in 1:1–2:4a is from the later Priestly tradition (so named because of the circles in which it arose). Neither account mentions or alludes to same-sex attraction or activity. Despite this, it is often alleged that what they say, respectively, about the creation of male and female (1:26-28) and the sexual attraction that brings man and woman together (2:20-24) rules out thinking of homosexuality as in any way compatible with God's intention and will. Such a claim, however, goes quite beyond anything the accounts themselves say or imply.

In the Priestly account (1:1–2:4a), creation is presented as God's bringing order to chaos through a process of separation and distinction. God creates, in turn, light and darkness, the waters above and the waters below, the earth and the seas, the sun and the moon, and so on. On the sixth day,

God said, "Let us make humankind in our image, according to our like-ness. . . ." So God created humankind in his image, / in the image of God he created them; / male and female he created them. / God blessed them, and God said to them, "Be fruitful and multiply, and fill the earth and sub-due it; and have dominion over the fish of the sea and over the birds of the air and over every living thing that moves upon the earth." (1:26-28)

Here "humankind" translates the Hebrew word *adam*, which refers to the whole of humanity. God's differentiating humankind as "male" and "female" (biological terms) and his blessing them to "be fruitful and mul-tiply" doesn't distinguish them from other living creatures. What sets them apart from all other beings is, rather, their creation in God's own "image" and "likeness." This gives them a special relationship to their Creator and, in turn, to all other creatures (see 1:28b).

The earlier account (2:4b-24) is less interested in the divine ordering of the cosmos and nature than in God's provisions for the well-being of creation and those who inhabit it. In keeping with this focus, human beings are designated not by the biological terms "male" and "female," but by the social terms "man" and "woman."

The man gave names to all cattle, and to the birds of the air, and to every animal of the field; but for the man there was not found a helper as his partner. So the LORD God caused a deep sleep to fall upon the man, and he slept; then he took one of his ribs and closed up its place with flesh. And the rib that the LORD God had taken from the man he made into a woman and brought her to the man. Then the man said,

"This at last is bone of my bones
   and flesh of my flesh;
this one shall be called Woman,
   for out of Man this one was taken."

Therefore a man leaves his father and his mother and clings to his wife, and they become one flesh. (vv. 20-24)

There is nothing here about marriage as such, or even about monogamy, and unlike Gen 1, there is no mention of procreation. In this account the woman is created because the man is lonely and in need of a companion. Remarkably, what makes her a fit companion is not that she is sexually different from the man, but that she is "bone of [his] bones and flesh of [his] flesh." It is, therefore, not specifically to produce offspring that a man is attracted to a woman and "they become one flesh." It is because they belong to each other and need each other. This account highlights the *relationship* of man and woman, not male and female sexuality.

There is, then, nothing in these accounts that can be reasonably understood as either endorsing or condemning same-sex relationships. Both accounts are *etiological*, in that they intend to explain why things are as they are—or, more exactly, why things are as they are *assumed* to be. The Priestly account seeks to explain why the world is constituted as it is and works as it does: why there are separate species and kinds of creatures, and why they are to be kept separate (thus the Priestly concern for ritual purity); why God created humankind as male and female (to "be fruitful and multiply"); and why the Sabbath day is different from the others and should be kept holy (because God rested on the seventh day). Similarly, the Yahwist's account seeks to explain why a man is so powerfully attracted to a woman and they become "one flesh." This point of view, of course, is that of a male-dominated society; nothing is said about the attraction of a woman to a man.

Finally, the kinds of considerations that are usually involved when one struggles with *moral* issues are not present in these accounts. No consideration is given to *variations* in nature, to *exceptional* conditions, or to *particular* circumstances. The Priestly account, for example, simply *presumes* that every human being is born with unambiguously male or female sex organs and is fully capable, physiologically, of having offspring. And the

Yahwistic account simply *presumes* that the desire for physical union with the opposite sex is universal. No attention is paid to those who are incapable of sexual relations or involuntarily deprived of them, to those who are voluntarily celibate, or to those whose erotic desires are for union with their own sex. These accounts provide no scriptural basis for the claim, frequently made, that homosexuality is inherently and unconditionally evil because it is a perversion of the created order.

Paul's World

Paul's thinking was shaped not only by his Jewish heritage and, of course, his life experiences. It was shaped also by his engagement with various religious and intellectual currents in the Greco-Roman world. It is, therefore, important to approach the apostle's references to same-sex activity with an awareness of what his contemporaries were saying on the topic. We shall consider the relevant sources that are representative of Hellenistic Judaism, Hellenistic moral philosophy, and emergent Christianity.

Hellenistic Judaism

Among the Jews of Paul's day, same-sex activity seems to have been less in evidence than in the ancient Mediterranean world as a whole. Indeed, Jews commonly named such conduct as a typical Gentile vice, one of the abhorrent perversions that results from idolatry. The contrast drawn between Jewish and pagan morality in a Jewish writing from the second century B.C.E. is typical:

> [Jews] are mindful of holy wedlock, and they do not engage in impious intercourse with male children, as do Phoenicians, Egyptians, and Romans, spacious Greece and many nations and others, Persians and

Galatians and all Asia, transgressing the holy law of immortal God, which they transgressed. (*Sibylline Oracles* 3.595-600)

Such accusations were also made by later rabbis, who regularly interpreted the Levitical prohibition of male same-sex intercourse as applying equally to females. A tale told by the Jewish historian Josephus (37–ca. 100 C.E.) shows that this stereotype of Gentiles was deep-seated in Jewish culture. He reports that when the Roman general Marc Antony (83–30 B.C.E.) asked Herod to send his young brother-in-law, Aristobulus, to Rome, Herod decided that it "would not be safe" because Antony might actually want to use the handsome youth "for erotic purposes" (*Jewish Antiquities* 15.6 §§28-29). Elsewhere, explaining Jewish marriage laws for the benefit of Gentile readers, Josephus speaks more directly of (male) same-sex activity:

> The law [of Moses] recognizes no sexual intercourse except the natural intercourse of man and wife, and this only for the procreation of children. It abhors sexual intercourse between males, and punishes with death anyone who is guilty of an assault. (*Against Apion* 2.24 §199, my translation)

This description of the intercourse between husband and wife as "natural" implies that same-sex intercourse is "unnatural," and later on in the same writing Josephus says that explicitly (2.37 §§273, 275). The same view surfaces regularly in other ancient Jewish sources. In the *Testament of Naphtali* (second century B.C.E.), for example, Sodom is mentioned as a case in point: "In the firmament, in the earth, and in the sea, in all the products of his workmanship discern the Lord who made all things, so that you do not become like Sodom, which departed from the order of nature" (3:4).

Jewish writers regarded same-sex intercourse to be a perversion of nature for two principal reasons: because no children can be born of such relationships, and because (it was presumed) same-sex partners, whether males or females, defile their true maleness or femaleness. The first reason is succinctly stated by the Jewish philosopher Philo (ca. 30 B.C.E.–45 C.E.): the man who lies with another man "pursues an unnatural pleasure and does his best to render cities desolate and uninhabited by destroying the means of procreation" (*Special Laws* 3.39). The second is found, for example, in a compilation of moral advice that dates from between 30 B.C.E. and 40 C.E.: "Do not transgress with unlawful sex the limits set by nature. For even animals are not pleased with intercourse of male with male. And let not women imitate the sexual role of men" (Pseudo-Phocylides, *Sentences* 190-92).

The warning here that women should not transgress the role of men is typical of the patriarchal, male-dominated cultures of the ancient world. This viewpoint is also operative when, as happens more often, and in accord with Lev 18:22 and 20:13, the males in a same-sex relationship are accused of shaming themselves. Philo, for example, claimed that such conduct "forces the male type of nature to debase and convert itself into the feminine form, just to indulge a polluted and accursed passion" (*Special Laws* 2.50).

Philo's embellishments of the biblical story of Lot and the men of Sodom provide further evidence of Jewish abhorrence of homosexual behavior. He describes the Sodomites as consumed by insatiable lusts and driven into all manner of excesses, including sexual. Corrupted by their opulence,

> they threw off from their necks the law of nature and applied them-
> selves to deep drinking of strong liquor and dainty feeding and forbid-
> den forms of intercourse. Not only in their mad lust for women did they
> violate the marriages of their neighbors, but also men mounted males

without respect for the sex nature which the active partner shares with the passive; and so when they tried to beget children they were discovered to be incapable of any but a sterile seed. Yet the discovery availed them not, so much stronger was the force of the lust that mastered them. Then, as little by little they accustomed those who were by nature men to submit to play the part of women, they saddled them with the formidable curse of a female disease. For not only did they emasculate their bodies by luxury and voluptuousness but they worked a further degeneration in their souls and, as far as in them lay, were corrupting the whole of mankind. (*On Abraham* 135-37)

Hellenistic Moral Philosophy

Homosexual relationships had a relatively prominent place in Greek society from the sixth century B.C.E. onward. As several historians have noted, this coincided with the development of a commercial economy based on the institution of slavery and the use of money in business transactions. It coincided also with the increasingly subordinate role that women played in Greek life. In this male-dominated society, even when the young female form became the model for beauty, the youthful male was regarded as embodying the ideal. Similarly, the Greek ideal of friendship was considered to be that between two free males of equal social standing. Male-female relationships could not realize this ideal, for females were regarded as inferior to males; and marriages were honored primarily for producing and nurturing children.

This was the sociocultural context within which the Greek practice of *pederasty* developed. A *pederast* (literally, "lover of boys") was an adult male who showered his attentions on attractive boys in their early teen years. Pederasty was often extolled by the philosophers as the purest form of love because it was not burdened, like the love between a man and his wife, with the goal of producing children. On the island of Crete it was thought shameful for a boy not to have a lover, a custom that may have derived from ancient puberty rites. In Boeotia, it was reported, men and boys paired off into actual marriages. But there was a dark side of pederasty, for the youth in such a relationship was highly vulnerable to the erotic demands of the older male and often a victim of sexual abuse. Thus, in Plato's *Phaedrus* (241) Socrates warns: "These things, dear boy, you must bear in mind, and you must know that the fondness of the lover is not a matter of goodwill, but of appetite which he wishes to satisfy: 'Just as the wolf loves the lamb, so the lover adores his beloved.' "

Pederasty was still practiced in the Greco-Roman world, and its merits were still sometimes argued in the philosophical literature. Increasingly, however, two other forms of pederasty claimed the attention of moral philosophers contemporary with Paul, evoking from most of them strong words of condemnation. One behavior condemned was the sexual exploitation of youthful male slaves by their masters, and another was the sale of sexual favors by teenage boys to older male clients. These would have been the types of male homoeroticism most evident in the urban centers of the Roman world, and the forms of which the apostle would have been most aware. The works of several writers of Paul's day suggest what he himself likely had in mind when he referred to same-sex conduct and why he too judged it to be reprehensible.

Seneca (already cited in ch. 2) was named a Roman praetor in 49 C.E. and simultaneously appointed tutor to the young Nero, whose mother was at that time married to the emperor, Claudius. When Nero succeeded Claudius five years later, Seneca became Nero's political adviser. In 62 C.E., disillusioned with Nero's policies, Seneca retired from public life. During his retirement, he wrote a series of essays in which he expressed concern about the lack of moral reason and responsibility in the Roman world. One evil that Seneca deplored was the exploitation of slaves by dissolute men of luxury. Seneca asked his readers to envision a banquet at which the youthful slave who serves the wine

> must dress like a woman and wrestle with his advancing years; he can-
> not get away from his boyhood; . . . he is kept beardless by having his
> hair smoothed away or plucked out by the roots, and he must remain
> awake throughout the night, dividing his time between his master's
> drunkenness and his lust. (*Moral Epistles* 47, "On Master and Slave," 7)

Here Seneca identifies homoerotic activity as driven by raw passion and involving the exploitation of a male slave who, by reason of his sub-servient position, is vulnerable to the degenerate whims and fantasies of his master. By being forced to dress like a woman and appear to be beard-less, he has been reduced to a mere object of erotic desire. Dandied up as a smooth-faced male, he embodies the ideal of beauty; attired as a woman, he embodies subservience and sexual vulnerability.

Plutarch (already cited in ch. 2) was a prolific Greek biographer, essay-ist, and moralist. He, too, provides helpful information about the social environment in which Paul's ministry was conducted. For several decades he served as a priest in the famed temple of Apollo in Delphi; he knew Athens well; and he had traveled in Egypt and lectured in Rome. In his *Dialogue on Love* he has several young men debate whether handsome young Bacchon should marry the rich widow of Thespiae, a certain Ismenodora. Anthemion and Pisias, rivals for Bacchon's affections, have been asked to decide. Anthemion, joined by his friend Daphnaeus, is for the marriage; but Pisias, joined by his friend Protogenes, is against it.

Pisias argues, against the marriage, that decent women are incapable of either receiving or giving sexual pleasure (752 B, C). Daphnaeus, on the other side, insists that "if union contrary to nature with males does not destroy or curtail a lover's tenderness, it stands to reason that the love between men and women, being normal and natural, will be conducive to friendship developing in due course from favour" (751 C). The same speaker goes on to argue that "to consort with males . . . is a completely ill-favoured favour, indecent, an unlovely affront to Aphrodite [the Greek goddess of love and fertility]" (751 D, E). In an aside, Daphnaeus distinguishes between male same-sex intercourse "without consent, in which case it involves violence and brigandage," and that which is "with consent," in which case "there is still weakness and effeminacy on the part of those who, contrary to nature, allow themselves in Plato's words 'to be covered and mounted like cattle.' "

Plutarch's dialogue shows that even consensual male homoeroticism could be viewed as exploitative and "contrary to nature." Concern for the violation of nature is also evident in the strong condemnation of same-sex intercourse found in the works of Dio Chrysostom (died after 112 C.E.). Banished from Rome early in the reign of Domitian (81–96 C.E.), Dio wandered for many years through Greece, the Balkans, and Asia Minor, preaching the views and values that were typical of the Stoics and Cynics of his day. Two particular features of homoerotic activity as he knew it stand out in his writings.

First, like Seneca, Dio saw homosexuality as essentially exploitative. In one place he refers to dissolute males

> who, although there are women in abundance, through wantonness and lawlessness wish to have females produced for them from males, and so they take boys and emasculate them. And thus a far worse and more unfortunate breed is created, weaker than the female and more effeminate. (*Discourse* 77/78, 36)

Elsewhere (*Discourse* 21, 6-10) he documents such wantonness by referring to the infamous relationship of Nero and his young male lover, Sporos, who dressed and wore his hair parted like a woman. After the death of Nero's second wife, Poppaea Sabina, the emperor ordered Sporos to be castrated, renamed him Sabina, and in 67 C.E. was publicly wed to him in a traditional ceremony of marriage.

Second, Dio understood homosexuality to be an expression of absolutely insatiable lust. In his Euboean discourse (*Discourse* 7) he identifies brothel keeping as an occupation that is legitimate for neither the rich nor the poor. Brothel keepers, he complains, "bring individuals together in union without love and intercourse without affection, and all for the sake of filthy lucre" (133). Like Daphnaeus in Plutarch's dialogue, Dio asserts that prostitution blasphemes the goddess Aphrodite, "whose name stands for the normal intercourse and union of the male and female" (135). Moreover, he argues, in cities where the young women are thus corrupted, the corruption of young men is likely to follow. He reasons that men will grow weary of satisfying their lust for women, especially when, for a fee, they have ready access to the town prostitutes. He warns:

> The man whose appetite is insatiate in such things, when he finds there is no scarcity, no resistance, in this field, will have contempt for the easy conquest and scorn for a woman's love, as a thing too readily given—in fact, too utterly feminine—and will turn his assault against the male quarters, eager to befoul the youth who will very soon be magistrates and judges and generals, believing that in them he will find a kind of pleasure difficult and hard to procure. (151-52)

In other words, Dio judged the raging lust that drives a man to seek intercourse with another male as but a more extreme expression of the same depravity that drives him to female prostitutes. He likens such a man to people addicted to wine who, when they eventually lose their taste for it, must "create an artificial thirst by the stimulus of sweatings, salted foods, and condiments" (152). Commenting on "Sexual Indulgence," Musonius (30–102 C.E.) expressed a similar judgment:

Not the least significant part of the life of luxury and self-indulgence lies also in sexual excess; for example those who lead such a life crave a variety of loves not only lawful but unlawful ones as well, not women alone but also men; sometimes they pursue one love and sometimes another, and not being satisfied with those which are available, pursue those which are rare and inaccessible, and invent shameful intimacies, all of which constitute a grave indictment of manhood. (12.1-10)

Dio and Musonius are typical of their age in regarding homoerotic sex as representing not simply an attraction to one's own sex rather than to the other, but "sexual excess" and uncontrolled passions.

Emergent Christianity

Paul's first contacts with the followers of Jesus were during his years as a Pharisee when, as he himself tells it, he "was violently persecuting the church of God and . . . trying to destroy it" (Gal 1:13). By the time he had embraced the gospel and embarked on his apostolic mission—most likely around the year 35 or shortly thereafter—the church already had a cadre of respected leaders who had been among Jesus' closest disciples, and various still-developing traditions that were formed in the course of its preaching, teaching, and worship. Whether we think of that earliest faith community as the Jesus movement, a designation preferred by many present-day scholars, or choose to speak simply of emergent Christianity, it is worth asking whether Paul's thinking about same-sex relationships could have been shaped in some way by earlier Christian views.

The traditions concerning Jesus were, of course, critically important for his followers as they sought to understand the significance of his death and resurrection and what they were now called to be and do. Chief among the Jesus-traditions were accounts of his crucifixion and of his resurrection appearances, but there were also accounts of his ministry and collections of his sayings and parables. We have access to these traditions only where they happen to be echoed or employed by later writers. Although Paul's letters (the earliest surviving Christian writings) offer some help in identifying them, we are dependent mainly on the gospels of Matthew and Mark, and the two-volume work, Luke–Acts.

The claim that Jesus was silent on the topic of homosexuality has to be qualified in several respects. As pointed out at the beginning of this chapter, the whole Bible is silent about homosexuality as this term is employed today. Indeed, if we replace the word *homosexuality* with some expression like *same-sex intercourse*, we can still speak of Jesus' silence on the subject. But even then, we can claim only that the *traditions* concerning Jesus say nothing about same-sex intercourse. There is no reason to suppose that all of his sayings have survived in those traditions. Moreover, the traditions do present Jesus as citing the very texts from Gen 1–2 that some invoke to condemn homosexuality as incompatible with the will of God. Before we look at those references, however, several other general observations need to be made about the Jesus-traditions.

1. The Levitical prohibition of male same-sex intercourse is neither cited nor echoed anywhere in the Jesus-traditions.

2. In a few instances Jesus mentions Sodom, alluding to the story in Gen 19 (Matt 10:15, parallel Luke 10:12; Matt 11:23-24; Luke 17:29). But in none of these instances are the residents of the city identified with any particular transgression. Only God's judgment and the city's destruction are in view. This is consistent with the way Sodom is usually represented in the Old Testament, as in Isa 1:9—Paul's citation of which (Rom 9:29) accounts for the only reference to the city in his letters.

3. A comment about "eunuchs" attributed to Jesus in Matt 19:11-12 has nothing to do with male same-sex relations. It occurs in Jesus' response to his disciples' suggestion that it may be "better not to marry" than to have to commit oneself to a marriage with no option for a divorce (v. 10):

He said to them, "Not everyone can accept this teaching, but only those to whom it is given. For there are eunuchs who have been so from birth, and there are eunuchs who have been made eunuchs by others, and there are eunuchs who have made themselves eunuchs for the sake of the kingdom of heaven." (vv. 11-12)

In other words, celibacy is appropriate only for those who have been born without the needed sexual organs, who have subsequently suffered their loss, or who have been "given" the ability to remain single for the purpose of serving God's kingdom more fully (compare Paul's view of celibacy, discussed in ch. 2 above).

4. Like Jesus' references to Sodom and eunuchs, his comments about creation have nothing to do with the subject of homosexuality. According to Mark 10:2-9 (parallel Matt 19:3-6),

> some Pharisees came, and to test [Jesus] they asked, "Is it lawful for a man to divorce his wife?" He answered them, "What did Moses command you?" They said, "Moses allowed a man to write a certificate of dismissal and to divorce her." But Jesus said to them, "Because of your hardness of heart he wrote this commandment for you. But from the beginning of creation, 'God made them male and female.' 'For this reason a man shall leave his father and mother and be joined to his wife, and the two shall become one flesh.' So they are no longer two, but one flesh. Therefore what God has joined together, let no one separate."

Here, passing over the provision for divorce contained in the law of Moses (Deut 24:1-4), Jesus calls on the creation accounts to show that divorce is in every case a perversion of the created order and thus always contrary to God's will. As in Gen 1–2, it is simply *assumed* that male and female were created for sexual union with each other. The question of same-sex unions is nowhere in view; it is a matter that lies completely beyond the scope of the Pharisees' question and Jesus' response.

As noted above, the silence of the Jesus-traditions about homoerotic conduct does not allow us to conclude that Jesus had nothing to say about this subject. Yet it does suggest that he had nothing *distinctive* to say about homoeroticism, pro or con; and also that this topic was of no special concern in the Christian communities where Jesus' teachings were being collected, interpreted, and applied.

Paul's Letters

The path we have been following toward Paul's letters has been a long one, but necessary. What the apostle says about homoerotic conduct—which is very little, indeed—can be best understood when we are aware of what he would have read in his Bible on this subject, of the forms that homoeroticism took in his own day, and of why it was condemned by many of his contemporaries, both Jewish and pagan. It is worth emphasizing, however, that despite the frequency with which Jewish and pagan writers took up the topic of homoerotic attraction and conduct, Paul's letters are the only Christian sources from the first century in which the topic surfaces. Moreover, we will see that the apostle never actually *addresses* homoeroticism as a topic in its own right, and that he never invokes the Genesis creation accounts, the story of the men of Sodom, or the rule in Lev 18:22 and 20:13 to support his implicit condemnation of same-sex intercourse. Only two passages in the certainly authentic Pauline letters, one in 1 Corinthians and one in Romans, need to claim our attention. As we turn to these passages, we need to keep several key points in mind.

1. In Paul's day, the critics of homoerotic activity invariably associated it with insatiable lust and avarice. Seneca portrayed it as a rich man's sport, Dio Chrysostom as the ultimate sexual debauchery, and Philo, with reference to Sodom, as one of the vile consequences of wanton luxury

and self-centeredness. The old Platonic ideal of the pure, disinterested love between a man and a boy had come to ruin on the hard realities of Roman decadence. One of the speakers in Plutarch's dialogue could acknowledge the possibility of genuine homosexual love, but even he saw a need to repeat Plato's warning about homoerotic seduction.

2. Although Paul's Bible and many of his contemporaries had much to say about sexual *conduct*, the ancient world had no conception of sexual *orientation*. Both Musonius and Dio Chrysostom, for instance, presumed that the same lusts that drove men to engage female prostitutes could drive them eventually to seduce other men. Similarly, Philo wrote of the Sodomites' sexual intercourse with men as if it were one form of their "mad lust for women." Moreover, all three of these writers presumed, with their contemporaries, that one could by force of will *control* these appetites and conform oneself to the prevailing cultural norms for sexual conduct.

3. In ancient Mediterranean societies, homoerotic relationships were widely regarded as a violation of the "natural" order. This judgment was based in part on the fact that same-sex intercourse produces no offspring. Primarily, however, homoerotic relationships were viewed as violating the cultural assumptions and expectations concerning male superiority. This is evident in the Levitical rule that prohibits a man lying with another male "as with a woman." It is equally evident when writers of Paul's day speak of the shame that is brought on a man who, like a woman, has sex with another man, and of women who insolently imitate men when they engage in homoerotic pleasuring. What was called a violation of nature was, in fact, a violation of culturally defined gender boundaries, and that was regarded as shaming and dishonoring the male and diminishing his manliness.

4. Homoerotic conduct was also commonly assumed to involve, necessarily, one person's exploitation of another. Plutarch's Daphnaeus

admitted that even if the passive male has consented to homoerotic inter-course, by taking on the "weakness" and "effeminacy" of a woman, his shame is greater than a woman's because he has surrendered his manli-ness. From this point of view, if there is exploitation of one person by another even where there is consent, how much more where there is none. One thinks of the Sodomites' attempted rape of Lot's visitors, of the sexual favors a master could demand of his slaves, and of a pederast's sexual abuse of a pubescent boy. To ethical teachers in the Greco-Roman world, it would have seemed just as obvious that homoerotic conduct was inherently exploitative as that it was driven by untamed lust.

1 Corinthians 6:9-11

This passage appears on the radar screens of those engaged with the topic of homosexuality only because of two words that stand, one after the other, in a list of people whom Paul identifies as unworthy of God's kingdom (vv. 9b-10a). Unfortunately, however, the translation of pre-cisely these two words is somewhat problematic.

In English alone, the first word (Greek: *malakoi*, a masculine plural adjective) has been variously rendered as "effeminate" (KJV; ASV); "catamites" (JB); "male prostitutes" (NIV, NRSV); "boy prostitutes" (NAB, 1986); "the self-indulgent" (NJB); and "a pervert" (CEV). The second (Greek: *arsenokoitai*, a masculine plural noun) has been translated as "abusers of themselves with mankind" (KJV), or ". . . with men" (ASV); "sodomites" (JB; NJB; NRSV); "homosexual offenders" (NIV); "practicing homosexuals" (NAB, 1986); and "a homosexual" (CEV). Moreover, and misleadingly, some versions have used just one expression to stand for the two words together: "homosexuals" (RSV, 1946); "homo-sexual perversion" (NEB); "homosexual perverts" (TEV); "sexual per-verts" (RSV, 1971); "sexual pervert" (REB); "sodomites" (NAB, 1970); and "male prostitutes" (NTPIV). It is worth noting that the first use of the word *homosexuals* in an English Bible (in 1 Cor 6:9b) was as recently as 1946, with the publication of the original edition of the Revised Standard Version.

Despite this rather astonishing range of translations, we can be reasonably confident about the *general* connotations of the words as they occur in this context. The basic meaning of the first one (*malakos*) is "softness" (used in this sense in Matt 11:8, parallel Luke 7:25) or "weakness" (the related noun means "sickness," e.g., Matt 4:23). Because ancient Mediterranean cultures regarded softness and weakness as typically female traits, the word was also applied, in a derogatory way, to "effeminate" males, and sometimes specifically to the receptive partner in same-sex intercourse, including male prostitutes fancied up for their trade.

The second word (*arsenokoitēs*), found in no source earlier than 1 Corinthians, is a compound of two words that mean, respectively, "male" and "bed." It could refer to "a male who lies [has sex] with a male" or to "a male who lies [has sex] with" either a male or a female. In this case the first meaning is likely because the word that immediately precedes it in 1 Cor 6:9b often has a homoerotic reference (as we have noted above). In addition, there is a good chance that Paul (or the source he used in drawing up this list of vices) was prompted to coin the term by the Greek version of Lev 20:13, where the words "male" and "bed" stand side by side (*arsenos koitēn*) in the rule against same-sex intercourse.

It is possible, then, to take *malakoi* as a reference to "male prostitutes" (e.g., NRSV) and *arsenokoitai* as a reference to males who pay to have sex with them. But it is equally possible, and probably better, to take the words as referring, respectively, to the "receptive" and "aggressive" males in any homoerotic encounter. We may therefore translate the first term as "effeminate males," and the second as "males who have sex with males." Our next task is to consider the context in which these references occur.

In 1 Cor 5 and 6, Paul is discussing various problems of sexual immorality, and beginning in chapter 7, as we have seen (above, ch. 2), he will
deal with several questions about sex and marriage that had been put to
him in a letter from Corinth. In chapters 5 and 6, however, he is responding, first, to troubling news that he had probably heard from the bearer of
that letter. Some unnamed man in the Corinthian congregation had
apparently been living with his stepmother, presumably now widowed
(5:1). Paul directs that the man should be put out of the church because
of his aberrant behavior (5:2-5). It seems that the Corinthian Christians
had not been very worried about the matter. Paul is astonished at their
smug complacency ("And you are arrogant!" 5:2), and he criticizes their
spiritual pride (5:6-8).

This specific case of sexual immorality in Corinth—we should note
that it involved heterosexual, not homosexual behavior—prompts Paul,
in 5:9-13, to clarify something he had said in an earlier letter (now lost).
There he had apparently warned the Corinthians not to associate with
persons guilty of any kind of immorality, sexual or otherwise (5:9). The
Corinthians had taken this to mean (or at least Paul thought they had
taken it to mean) that they needed to withdraw from society in order to
protect themselves from its evils. Not at all, says Paul; that is quite impossible (5:10). He meant, rather, that they should break off fellowship with
other Christians whose conduct, like that of the man living with his stepmother, threatened the moral integrity of the whole believing community
(5:11-13).

Paul's instruction to the Corinthians about disciplining errant members of their congregation moves him, in 6:1-11, to comment on the
impropriety of Christians taking their disputes to secular judicatories for
settlement. Of course, it is a shame that any such disputes even arise
within the church (6:7-8), but if they do, they should also be heard and
settled there, not before "unbelievers" (6:6). Implicit in the argument of

these verses is the apostle's conviction that Christians do not belong, ultimately, to this age—they are presently in the world (see 5:10) but they are not "of" it. Paul identifies those who belong to the world as "unbelievers" (6:6) and, later, as "wrongdoers" (6:9), while he identifies Christians as "saints," people set apart for the service of God (6:1, 2). The question "Do you not know that wrongdoers will not inherit the kingdom of God?" (6:9a) emphasizes and extends this distinction between believers and unbelievers. On the one hand, there are the "saints" who *belong to God's kingdom* even while they are in this world; on the other hand, there are the "unbelievers" or "unrighteous" people who *belong to this world*, insofar as they submit to its claims and not to God's.

In 6:9b-10, to make this point more concrete, Paul offers ten examples of "wrongdoers" who belong to this world rather than to God's kingdom. The list is similar to those in 5:10-11, in other Pauline letters (e.g., Rom 1:29-31; Gal 5:19-21), and elsewhere in the New Testament (e.g., Mark 7:21-22; 1 Pet 4:3, 15; Rev 9:21; 21:8; 22:15), but no two of them are identical. Paul would have been acquainted with many similar lists in the moral literature of Hellenistic Judaism. And his lists, in turn, were certainly known to later writers, including the author of the Pastoral Epistles who, decades later, wrote in Paul's name (see below, ch. 4). This perhaps accounts for the inclusion of the word *arsenokoitēs* in 1 Tim 1:9-10, the only place it is to be found in the New Testament apart from 1 Cor 6:9b.

Paul and others who employed lists of this sort assembled them more or less at random from well-known ethical traditions. The intention was not to offer a comprehensive catalog of all or even the chief evils to be avoided. This is evident, for example, when Paul closes a list in Galatians with the phrase "and things like these" (5:21). As a rule, the apostle, like other Jews, lists vices that he associated particularly with Gentile idolaters, and this is clearly the case in 1 Cor 6:9b-10. He is no doubt thinking of the pagan background of the majority of Corinthian Christians when he reminds them, "This is what some of you used to be" (6:11a). However, their baptism into Christ has now marked them as persons who have been transformed by God's righteousness and God's Spirit, and set apart for God's service.

Clearly, same-sex intercourse is not Paul's topic in 1 Cor 5 and 6. The sexual immorality that he specifically addresses in these chapters is heterosexual, not homosexual. There is, first of all, the case of the man living with his stepmother (ch. 5), and then a warning addressed to the men of the congregation that they should not patronize female prostitutes (6:12-20). While Paul appears to use two terms that refer to participants in homoerotic intercourse, these are merely listed, along with a number of other "wrongdoers" ("fornicators, idolaters, adulterers, . . . thieves, the greedy, drunkards, revilers, robbers"), as a reminder to his congregation that, as believers, they have been graced with a new way of life.

Given the context, we learn only one thing about Paul's view of homoerotic conduct: men who engage in it are thereby disqualified from participation in the kingdom of God. He does not bother to indicate whether the same applies to females who engage in such conduct (we shall presently see that he believed it does). Nor does he offer any *reasons* why males should not have sex with males. Like other writers, he lists behaviors that he assumes all decent people will agree are wrong. Paul does not, either here or elsewhere, call such vices sins, however. Whenever the plural form *sins* appears in his letters, it is either a quotation from Scripture (once) or in a more or less set formula that he has taken over from church traditions (four times). The apostle himself viewed sin (singular) both as a power that drives a wedge between God and humankind and as the condition of alienation from God that results. He regarded specific vices, like the ones that he lists here and elsewhere, as *symptomatic* of sin, not as its essence. This important point becomes especially clear when we turn to a passage in Romans.

Romans 1:24-27

On any reckoning, Romans was written several years after 1 Corinthians. But unlike the earlier letter, Romans was addressed to a Christian community (likely organized into several house churches) that was not of the apostle's founding. He had never been as far west as Italy. One of his reasons for writing Romans was to gain support for a mission to Spain that he hoped to launch from the imperial city with the help of the Roman Christians. The passage that bears on our topic occurs close to the beginning of this letter (Rom 1:24-27):

> Therefore God gave [idolaters] up in the lusts of their hearts to impurity, to the degrading of their bodies among themselves, because they exchanged the truth about God for a lie and worshiped and served the creature rather than the Creator, who is blessed forever! Amen. For this reason God gave them up to degrading passions. Their women exchanged natural intercourse for unnatural, and in the same way also the men, giving up natural intercourse with women, were consumed with passion for one another. Men committed shameless acts with men and received in their own persons the due penalty for their error.

This paragraph contains the only biblical reference to *female* homo-eroticism (v. 26b) and leaves us in no doubt that the apostle associates all homoerotic conduct with the "degrading passions" and "shameless acts" that follow from idolatry. We must not, however, isolate these verses from their context. The very first word in verse 24, "therefore," translates a (Greek) coordinating conjunction, and this, if nothing else, requires us to take stock of the preceding paragraphs. What is Paul's topic in this section of the letter? What are his aim and the logic of his argument? What prompts him to mention homoerotic conduct?

We may begin with the observation that Paul has not formulated his reference to homoerotic relationships as a moral directive, and that it does not stand in the section of the letter where most of his ethical appeals and exhortations are to be found (chs. 12–15). Nor does it occur in the sections where he is introducing the Roman Christians to his understanding of the gospel (3:21–8:39; chs. 9–11). It occurs, rather, in a section (1:18–3:20) where his aim is to show that the whole of humankind, Jew and Gentile alike, have sinned and fallen short of the glory of God (see 3:22b-23); and, therefore, that all are in need of being put right (justified) by God's saving grace. Paul speaks first of sin's power as it is manifested among the Gentiles (1:18-32), and later of sin's power as it is manifested among the Jews (2:17–3:20). The paragraphs in between (2:1-16) emphasize the impartiality of God, who causes "anguish and distress for *everyone* who does evil" and provides "glory and honor and peace for *everyone* who does good" (vv. 9-11, italics added).

The indictment of the Gentiles in 1:18-32 contains terms and arguments that were the stock-in-trade of much Hellenistic-Jewish teaching, although Paul has adapted and configured these in his own way. He allows that the Gentiles, even though they have not been, like the Jews, "instructed in the law" (see 2:18), are nonetheless able to know about God as he discloses himself in creation "through the things he has made" (vv. 19-20a). In Paul's view, however, knowledge *about* God is not enough to qualify as faith in God. He declares the Gentiles to be "without excuse" because "though they knew God, they did not honor him as God or give thanks to him" (vv. 20b-21a). Instead, "they became futile in their thinking, and their senseless minds were darkened. Claiming to be wise, they became fools; and they exchanged the glory of the immortal God for images resembling a mortal human being or birds or four-footed animals or reptiles" (vv. 21b-23).

Even though words for "sin" do not occur until later (the verb in 2:12, the noun in 3:9), Paul's understanding of sin is elegantly stated in 1:21a:

sin is refusing to give God glory (NRSV: "honor") and thanks, which is to say, it is refusing to acknowledge the grace and the claim that underlie and give order to the whole of creation.

In the case of the Gentiles, sin is manifested as idolatry. When "they exchanged the glory of the immortal God for images" that looked like themselves or birds or animals (v. 23, echoing Ps 106:20, which refers to *Israel's* idolatry), they had, in fact, "exchanged the truth about God for a lie" and devoted themselves to "the creature rather than the Creator" (v. 25). This confusion of creature and Creator is not just "theological" in character but also "moral," because to turn away from the Creator (sin) is to turn away, as well, from the moral order of creation. Paul's reasoning here corresponds to the attacks on idolatry that were typical of the literature of Hellenistic Judaism. For example, the Wisdom of Solomon (a first-century B.C.E. book included in the Septuagint) attributes all manner of evils to the Gentiles' ignorance of God:

> For whether they kill children in their initiations, or celebrate secret
>   mysteries,
> or hold frenzied revels with strange customs,
> they no longer keep either their lives or their marriages pure,
> but they either treacherously kill one another, or grieve one another by
>   adultery,
> and all is a raging riot of blood and murder, theft and deceit, corruption,
>   faithlessness, tumult, perjury,
> confusion over what is good, forgetfulness of favors,
> defiling of souls, sexual perversion,
> disorder in marriages, adultery, and debauchery.
> For the worship of idols not to be named
> is the beginning and cause and end of every evil. (14:23-27)

This passage sheds light on the function of Rom 1:24-32. Like the unknown author of the Wisdom of Solomon, Paul is illustrating the moral chaos that follows from idolatry. The vices he mentions are among those that Jews typically attributed to Gentiles and are meant to be representative of "every kind of wickedness" (v. 29). He does not call them sins but lists them as the consequences of the fundamental sin of idolatry, penalties appropriate for those who "did not see fit to acknowledge God" (v. 28).

Given the illustrative function of verses 24-32 within the argument of Rom 1:18-32, it is not surprising that Paul offers no particular reason for mentioning homoerotic conduct as an example of the moral chaos that follows from the refusal to let God be God. But why does he give relatively more attention to homoerotic behavior than to the vices he merely lists in verses 29-31 ("covetousness, malice . . . envy, murder, strife, deceit," etc.)? Why does he not simply mention it as one vice among others, as he had in 1 Cor 6:9? An important clue is his repeated use of "exchange," which occurs three times within just a few lines (vv. 23, 25, 26). He apparently found same-sex intercourse to be an especially apt illustration of the moral confusion to which idolatry leads: when the creature has been *exchanged* for the Creator (v. 23) and the truth about God has been *exchanged* for a lie (v. 25), who can be surprised that "natural intercourse" will be *exchanged* for "unnatural" (vv. 26-27)?

Paul doesn't say, however, *why* he believes that homoerotic sex is against nature, shameless, and evidence of dishonorable passions and burning lust. He assumes that the believers in Rome will know what he means and fully agree. Indeed, the language he uses here is similar and in several instances identical to the language used by others in his day when denouncing homoerotic relationships. It is, therefore, reasonable to suppose that the picture of homoerotic conduct Paul had in his mind corresponded closely to its depiction that we have seen in the literature of Hellenistic Judaism (e.g., Philo and Pseudo-Phocylides), and in the works of numerous Hellenistic moral philosophers (e.g., Seneca, Musonius, and

Dio Chrysostom). Like others, Paul regarded homoeroticism as a violation of the created order. Like others, he assumed that one simply decides to abandon "natural" intercourse ("exchanged" [v. 26] and "giving up" [v. 27] imply willful choice). And like others, he viewed this choice as driven by degraded desires and uncontrolled lust. A man of antiquity, he was as unaware as his contemporaries of the complex factors, including biological, that contribute to the shaping of sexual orientation.

In short, the attitude toward same-sex intercourse that surfaces in Rom 1:24-27 was widespread in Paul's day. Like many others, both Jews and pagans, the apostle was repulsed by such behavior. He provided neither reasoned arguments nor scriptural authorization for his view, presumably because he regarded homoerotic acts as self-evidently evil. What distinguishes this passage is not what Paul has said about homoerotic behavior but the context within which he has said it. The "bad news" about the human predicament spelled out in Rom 1:18–3:20—the whole of humankind has sinned and fallen short of God's glory—is but the run-up to an exposition of the "good news" that begins in Rom 3:21. The good news is that "God proves his love for us in that while we still were sinners Christ died for us" (5:8), and that absolutely nothing "will be able to separate us from the love of God in Christ Jesus our Lord" (8:39). This gospel of the gracious, saving love of God in Christ is the one great theme of all of Paul's letters and the fundamental theological basis of all of his moral reasoning and instruction.

Observations and Reflections

Our examination of representative ancient sources, including two specific passages in Paul's letters, has shown that the apostle, strictly speaking, said nothing about *homosexuality*. As noted earlier, this and related terms (including *heterosexuality* and *bisexuality*) were coined only in the latter half of the nineteenth century during the early phases of research into *sexual orientation*, of which there was no conception in the ancient world. The *physiology of sex, sexual desire,* and *sexual conduct* were all matters of discussion, but sexual orientation could not have been a topic for any ancient writer, including Paul. For this reason, the actual subject of the present chapter has not been Paul's view of homosexuality, but his view of *homoerotic conduct*. The following points need to be kept in mind, especially by those who are tempted to cite Pauline texts as providing unambiguous scriptural proof that homosexuality and all homosexual activity are inherently degenerate, disordered, and degrading.

1. *There are only two passages in Paul's letters where the matter of homoerotic conduct is even briefly in view, and it is not a topic of moral instruction or exhortation in either one of them.* The list of wrongdoers in 1 Cor 6:9b-10a includes two words that appear to refer, respectively, to the penetrated and penetrating partners in male same-sex intercourse, but Paul neither highlights them nor explains them. And even in Rom 1:26-27, where homoeroticism is given more attention, it is not Paul's subject.

2. *The apostle's references to same-sex intercourse have to be interpreted in the light of the wider theological contexts in which they stand.* This is especially true of Rom 1:26-27. There homoeroticism is but one of the vices that Paul names in his indictment of the Gentiles (1:18-32), and this indictment is, in turn, part of a larger section of "bad news" (1:18–3:20) that prepares for the "good news" to follow (3:21–8:39). When this context is taken into account, it becomes evident that Paul identifies homoerotic conduct as an especially obvious example—at least to him and the recipients of this letter—of the moral chaos that has been visited on humankind by reason of sin, which he regards as the refusal to acknowledge that life is God's gift and that one's existence stands always under God's claim.

3. Paul's denunciation of homoerotic conduct appears to have had no distinctively Christian roots, and there is no evidence that he sought to support his views on the subject with any particular scriptural or theological arguments. To the contrary, both the substance and the language of his references to homoeroticism suggest that his attitude toward it had been significantly shaped by prevailing cultural norms and stereotypes, including those that were part of his Jewish upbringing and education. In particular, the widespread condemnation of same-sex intercourse in the ancient Mediterranean world was based on three significant presuppositions (see above, "Paul's Bible" and "Paul's World").

First, it was commonly presupposed that all human beings are erotically attracted to the opposite sex, and that the true and proper reason for this attraction is the propagation of the species.

Again, it was commonly presupposed that all homoerotic sex is against nature (Rom 1:26, "natural intercourse for unnatural") because it violates the male's superior and dominant role in relation to the female. The reasoning was that a man who, like a woman, submits to penetration by another male is surrendering his manliness, that the man who penetrates him is complicit, and that both have shamed themselves by failing to exercise dominance over a woman. And sex between females was denounced because imitating the male's role amounted to a challenge of male superiority. Because this violation of gender roles was understood to dishonor especially the male (Rom 1:27, "Men committed shameless acts with men"), it was widely viewed as undermining the patriarchal and hierarchical structures of the political order and of society as a whole.

Finally, it was commonly presupposed that all homoerotic sex, consensual or not, is the wild raging of inordinate passions and lusts, the wanton indulgence of one's sexual appetites (Rom 1:24-27, "lusts . . . degrading passions . . . consumed with passion").

None of these presuppositions, and none of the stereotypes that went with them, has stood the test of time. More than a century of research in the biological, social, and behavioral sciences has taught us that human sexuality involves much more than physiology, erotic desire, and conduct. The presuppositions about homoeroticism that shaped the views of ancient writers are now as outdated as many of their judgments about human anatomy and the human reproductive system. Especially because of the knowledge that has been gained about *sexual orientation* and the complex factors that are involved in its formation, the ancient presuppositions about sex and gender have been rendered obsolete.

4. *To the extent that Paul's letters can inform discussions of homosexuality in our day, they will do so not because of what the apostle had to say about homoerotic conduct but because of what he had to say about the gospel he had been called to proclaim.* His two references to same-sex intercourse can be appreciated as part of his *rhetorical strategy* in 1 Cor 6 and Rom 1, respectively. They are not, however, among the core affirmations and claims that are definitive of his gospel. The affirmations at the heart of his gospel are that humankind is the creation of a just, loving, and faithful God, made in God's image as it is revealed in Christ; and that humankind, defiantly refusing to honor and give thanks to God, is being redeemed, renewed, and restored by God's unconditional love. For Paul, the decisive enactment of God's justice and love is Christ's reconciling death and resurrection. He understood that saving event to have inaugurated a "new creation" (2 Cor 5:14-17; Gal 6:15-16), and to have exposed all "human wisdom" as foolishness and everything deemed powerful by "human standards" as weakness (e.g., 1 Cor 1:23-31).

The gospel as it is articulated by Paul cannot and does not provide ready-made, once-and-for-all answers to questions about good and bad, right and wrong, justice and injustice. Rather, Paul's good news that the whole of creation has been graced and claimed by God's redeeming love is simultaneously a challenge to all of our imperfect, human notions of what is true and just and good, and a summons to be continually questioning and reassessing all of our presuppositions, all of our stereotypes, every cultural norm, and every social convention.

For Further Reading

Quotations in this chapter: "Draft Addition (December 2004)" to the entry on "Sexuality" in the *Oxford English Dictionary* (2nd ed., 1989), online: dictionary.oed.com; Phyllis A. Bird, "The Bible in Christian Ethical Deliberation concerning Homosexuality: Old Testament Contributions," in *Homosexuality, Science, and the "Plain Sense" of Scripture* (ed. David L. Balch; Grand Rapids: Eerdmans, 2000), 142–76.

Ancient sources cited in this chapter: the *Sibylline Oracles*, the *Testament of Naphtali*, and *Sentences* of Pseudo-Phocylides are cited from the translations in James H. Charlesworth, ed., *The Old Testament Pseudepigrapha* (2 vols.; Garden City, N.Y.: Doubleday, 1983); Dio Chrysostom, Josephus, Philo, Plato, Plutarch, and Seneca are cited, except as noted, from the translations in the Loeb Classical Library (Cambridge, Mass.: Harvard University Press, various years); Musonius is cited from Cora E. Lutz, "Musonius Rufus: The Roman Socrates," in *Yale Classical Studies* 10 (ed. A. R. Bellinger; New Haven, Conn.: Yale University Press, 1947), 32–147.

In addition to the volume edited by David L. Balch (above), the following books contain essays, contributed by authors of various viewpoints, that are pertinent to an understanding of the texts and issues discussed in this chapter: Robert L. Brawley, ed., *Biblical Ethics & Homosexuality: Listening to Scripture* (Louisville: Westminster John Knox, 1996); Jeffrey S. Siker, ed., *Homosexuality in the Church: Both Sides of the*

Debate (Louisville: Westminster John Knox, 1994); Choon-Leong Seow, ed., *Homosexuality and Christian Community* (Louisville: Westminster John Knox, 1996).

Other significant discussions of the texts and issues discussed in this chapter: John H. Elliott, "No Kingdom of God for Softies? or, What Was Paul Really Saying? 1 Corinthians 6:9-10 in Context," *Biblical Theology Bulletin* 34 (2004): 17–40; Martti Nissinen, *Homoeroticism in the Biblical World: A Historical Perspective* (trans. Kirsi Stjerna; Minneapolis: Fortress, 1998); Dale B. Martin, *Sex and the Single Savior*, listed with the "Further Reading" at the end of chapter 2.

Commentaries on Romans: Leander E. Keck, *Romans* (Abingdon New Testament Commentaries; Nashville: Abingdon Press, 2005); John Reumann, "Romans," in *Eerdmans Commentary on the Bible* (ed. J. D. G. Dunn and J. W. Rogerson; Grand Rapids, and Cambridge, U.K.: Eerdmans, 2003), 1277–1313; N. T. Wright, "The Letter to the Romans," in *The New Interpreter's Bible* 10 (ed. L. E. Keck et al.; Nashville: Abingdon Press, 2000), 393–770. More detailed: Brendan Byrne, *Romans* (Sacra Pagina; Collegeville, Minn.: Liturgical Press, 1996); Robert Jewett, *Romans: A Commentary* (Hermeneia; Minneapolis: Fortress, 2007).

Commentaries on 1 Corinthians are listed with the "Further Reading" at the end of chapter 2.

CHAPTER 4

WOMEN IN THE CHURCH

Our examination of Paul's references to marriage (ch. 2) disclosed that he regarded marriage partners as mutually responsible for the quality of their relationship. We have seen that it is
difficult to find real parallels to this emphasis in the writings of his contemporaries, either Jewish or non-Jewish. Now in this present chapter we
must ask whether Paul holds any corresponding view about the status of
men and women within the life and ministry of the church. For in many
Protestant denominations and in Roman Catholicism, the role of women
within the church continues to be problematic. Even in denominations
where the ordination of women does not continue to be questioned on
scriptural grounds, women clergy have often found the opportunities for
ministry more limited for them than for their male counterparts.

There seems little chance that the Vatican's long-standing refusal to
ordain women as priests or deacons will be changed any time soon. Pope
Benedict XVI has on various occasions affirmed the view set forth by his
predecessor, John Paul II, in the Apostolic Letter *Ordinatio Sacerdotalis*
(1994): "I declare that the Church has no authority whatsoever to confer
priestly ordination on women and that this judgment is to be definitively
held by all the Church's faithful." John Paul grounded this view, as had

popes before him, on "the Lord's way of acting in choosing the twelve men whom he made the foundation of his Church." Citing 1 Tim 3:1-13, 2 Tim 1:6, and Titus 1:5-9, he claimed further that "the Apostles did the same when they chose fellow workers who would succeed them in their ministry." So while it is true that the Vatican has called for expanding the responsibilities of women in the Catholic Church, it continues to exclude women from being ordained for either priestly or diaconal responsibilities.

Scriptural support is also claimed for the similar position staked out by the Southern Baptist Convention, the largest Protestant denomination in North America: "While both men and women are gifted for service in the church, the office of pastor is limited to men as qualified by Scripture." Consistent with this view, one of this denomination's seminaries refused tenure to a female professor, asserting that Scripture forbids women from teaching in the church. And a prominent Southern Baptist theologian (R. A. Mohler) warns that the "feminization of the ministry is one of the most significant trends of this generation," reversing "centuries of Christian conviction and practice." He goes on to claim that

> the issues of women's ordination and the normalization of homosexuality are closely linked. It is no accident that those churches that most eagerly embraced the ordination of women now either embrace the ordination of homosexuals or are seriously considering such a move.
>
> The reason for this is quite simple. The interpretive games one must play in order to get around the Bible's proscription of women in congregational preaching and teaching roles are precisely the games one must play in order to get around the Bible's clear condemnation of homosexuality.

On this subject, as on the others we are surveying, the authority of Paul has frequently been invoked, especially by those who argue that women should not be accorded equal status with men in the church's ministry.

In Dallas, for example, a church that belongs to a denomination in which local congregations decide who shall be ordained was proposing to ordain a woman into the ministry. Just before the final vote, one of its members arose to argue that it was not a proper role for a woman to have. He based his case primarily on the teaching of Paul, including the eleventh chapter of 1 Corinthians. There, he declared, "Paul had set up roles for the kingdom of God" by describing God as the head of Christ, Christ as the head of man, and a man as the head of a woman. "These roles," he went on,

> were not culturally conditioned, but were begun with Adam and Eve. The roles for men and women are not the same and it is no disgrace or shame to either sex that their roles are different. The church structure is set up by God in line with the family structure. As Christ is head over the church and as the husband is head over the family, so men are to be the authorities in the body of believers.

He cited several other texts as well, including 1 Cor 14:34 ("women should be silent in the churches") and 1 Tim 2:12 ("I permit no woman to teach or to have authority over a man; she is to keep silent").

The same position was taken by a Protestant minister in Kentucky who conducted a weekly question-and-answer column in the local newspaper. In response to a reader's query, he declared—citing 1 Timothy—that women are to have no major leadership roles in the church as a whole, including no part in preaching, teaching, (solo) music, or prayer when men are present. When women assume such roles, he concluded, "they violate the positive command of God through Paul."

These examples reflect the sacred-cow view of Paul's moral teaching that is characterized and critiqued in the opening chapter of this book. They also illustrate how seriously the Apostle's teaching on practical matters is distorted if one does not take account of all the evidence available to interpret it within the context of his gospel, his ministry, and his time and place.

The Problem of Sources

As observed above (ch. 1), we "find Paul"—we are able to engage his thought most directly—in the seven letters that can be accepted as his own. These are the writings on which we shall continue to focus as we consider his view of women in the church. At the outset, however, we need to pay attention to several non-Pauline passages that have given rise to many of the false ideas about the Apostle's views on this topic.

1 Timothy 2:8-15

New Testament scholarship, by and large, has concluded that 1 and 2 Timothy and Titus (commonly identified as Pastoral Epistles) were probably written in the early second century by someone (certainly a man, not a woman) who was concerned about preaching and practices that he regarded as subversive of true Christianity. To gain authority for his warnings and appeals, he represented them as Paul's. The teaching he opposed seems to have involved claims about the need for special religious knowledge, a negative view of the material world, the practice of asceticism, the belief that salvation means escaping from the world, and a "spiritualized" view of resurrection. According to the author of the Pastoral Epistles, this teaching was particularly attractive to the women of the Christian community; its proponents, he says, "make their way into households and captivate silly women" (2 Tim 3:6), "upsetting whole families by teaching for sordid gain what it is not right to teach" (Titus 1:11).

Those who cite 1 Tim 2:8-15 as scriptural authorization for their belief that women are unfit to be teachers or ministers of the gospel either ignore or dismiss as irrelevant the historical and ideological setting of these three writings. They also fail to see that this author—unlike the real Paul, who lived at least half a century earlier—accepted uncritically the prevailing cultural norms concerning the nature of women and their proper role in society. He is clearly reflecting those norms when he indicates his wish

> that the women should dress themselves modestly and decently in suitable clothing, not with their hair braided, or with gold, pearls, or expensive clothes, but with good works, as is proper for women who profess reverence for God. Let a woman learn in silence with full submission. I permit no woman to teach or to have authority over a man; she is to keep silent. For Adam was formed first, then Eve; and Adam was not deceived, but the woman was deceived and became a transgressor. Yet she will be saved through childbearing, provided they continue in faith and love and holiness, with modesty. (1 Tim 2:9-15)

In the Greco-Roman world generally, it was simply taken for granted that women should groom themselves modestly and conduct themselves with quiet restraint in the public sphere, in most respects submitting themselves to the supposedly wiser and abler leadership of men. Women who did not follow these conventions were often presumed to be women of easy virtue or else on the way to becoming such.

The teachings of two moral philosophers roughly contemporary with the author of the Pastoral Epistles are typical. According to Epictetus (ca. 55–130 C.E.),

> Immediately after they are fourteen, women are called "ladies" by men. And so when they see that they have nothing else but only to be the bedfellows of men, they begin to beautify themselves, and put all their hopes on that. It is worth while for us to take pains, therefore, to make them understand that they are honoured for nothing else but only for appearing modest and self-respecting. (*Encheiridion*, 40)

And Plutarch (already quoted in chs. 2 and 3) believed that what makes a woman beautiful "is not gold or precious stones or scarlet," but "dignity, good behaviour, and modesty" (*Advice to Bride and Groom*, 141.26). In addition, he argued that a woman's speech can be as seductive as her physical appearance:

> Not only the arm of the virtuous woman, but her speech as well, ought to be not for the public, and she ought to be modest and guarded about saying anything in the hearing of outsiders, since it is an exposure of herself; for in her talk can be seen her feelings, character and disposition. (*Advice*, 142.31)

It therefore follows, according to Plutarch, that a "woman ought to do her talking either to her husband or through her husband" (*Advice*, 142.32).

Similar views were current in Jewish circles. The *Testament of Reuben* (ca. second century B.C.E.) maintained that

> women are more easily overcome by the spirit of promiscuity than are men. They contrive in their hearts against men, then by decking themselves out they lead men's minds astray, by a look they implant their poison, and finally in the act itself they take them captive. For a woman is not able to coerce a man overtly, but by a harlot's manner she accomplishes her villainy. Accordingly, my children, flee from sexual promiscuity, and order your wives and daughters not to adorn their heads and their appearances so as to deceive men's sound minds. (5:3-5)

Along the same lines, the *Letter of Aristeas* (written sometime between 250 B.C.E. and 100 C.E.) advised men to recognize "that the female sex is bold, positively active for something which it desires, easily liable to change its mind because of poor reasoning powers, and of naturally weak constitution" (250). And in commenting on the biblical story of Adam and Eve, Philo (already quoted in ch. 3) claimed that a woman is more readily deceived than a man:

For [man's] judgment, like his body, is masculine and is capable of dissolving or destroying the designs of deception; but the judgment of woman is more feminine, and because of softness she easily gives way and is taken in by plausible falsehoods which resemble the truth. (*Questions and Answers on Genesis 1*, 33)

It is apparent, then, that the comments about women in 1 Tim 2:8-15 reflect certain values and customs of both Hellenistic and Jewish culture. We shall also see that the views expressed in this passage are very far from Paul's own, as those are disclosed in the unquestionably genuine letters. For example, and contrary to 1 Tim 2:14 ("Adam was not deceived"), the apostle himself identified Adam as the first and primary transgressor in Rom 5:12-21 and 1 Cor 15:21-22 (although he also spoke of Eve's being deceived, 2 Cor 11:3). And given his conviction that the end of history was near, one cannot imagine Paul declaring that a woman "will be saved through childbearing" (1 Tim 2:15; similarly 5:14). Still other differences from the apostle's views will become apparent below.

In sum the instructions about women in 1 Tim 2:8-15 should not be attributed to Paul himself. We still have to reckon with them, of course. But they need to be assessed with reference to the historical context and religious concerns of a man who was writing long after Paul's death. In particular, this writer's claim that women are saved by bearing children and dutifully fulfilling their domestic responsibilities was aimed at repudiating an ascetic form of Christianity that regarded sex, marriage, and family as incompatible with the life of faith.

Colossians and Ephesians

Most scholars who identify Colossians and Ephesians as deutero-Pauline letters, which is the view adopted in this book (above, ch. 1), identify Colossians as the earlier of the two and Ephesians as written by someone who knew and drew on Colossians. The two writings thus have much in common, both in form and in content. Although neither includes any counsels about the role of women in the church, they are often cited in confirmation of the view that women are to be subordinate to men in all ways and in every sphere of activity, including the church. The texts quoted are Col 3:18 ("Wives, be subject to your husbands, as is fitting in the Lord") and Eph 5:22, 24, 33 ("Wives, be subject to your husbands as you are to the Lord . . . in everything"; "and a wife should respect [literally: *fear, stand in awe of*] her husband"). As we have previously seen, the assignment of women to a subordinate status was in accord with the sociocultural norms of the Greco-Roman world.

The instructions to wives in Ephesians and Colossians stand within passages that scholars describe as "tables of household duties" or "household codes." These codes identify not only the responsibilities of wives to their husbands but also the responsibilities of husbands to their wives (Eph 5:25-33; Col 3:19), children to their parents (Eph 6:1-3; Col 3:20), parents to their children (Eph 6:4; Col 3:21), slaves to their masters (Eph 6:5-8; Col 3:22-25), and masters to their slaves (Eph 6:9; Col 4:1). No member of the household is without responsibility, and the well-being of the household is understood to depend on each one fulfilling his or her proper role. There is, however, a significant difference between these directives and what Paul had said about the mutual responsibilities of partners in a marriage (1 Cor 7:3-5). The apostle had called for exactly *the same thing* from the husband and the wife: a total sharing of oneself with the spouse. He had expressed this as yielding the right to exercise authority over oneself. In Colossians and Ephesians, however, where wives are instructed to "be subject" to husbands (Col 3:18; Eph 5:22, 24, 33), there is no equivalent directive to husbands. The husband's duty is not to recognize her authority over him but to love her ("as himself") and to care for her (Col 3:18; Eph 5:23, 28, 33; see also

1 Pet 3:1-7). Although the code in Ephesians is opened with a general appeal to "be subject to *one another*" (v. 21), that principle is immediately abandoned when the husband's role in a marriage is likened to the role of Christ: "The husband is the head of the wife just as Christ is the head of the church" (v. 23). Here a social norm (the husband as head of the household) has been given a theological (specifically christological) warrant.

In the ethical codes of such writings as Ephesians, Colossians, and 1 Peter, just as in the rules and regulations of the Pastoral Epistles, we see a concern for institutions and structures—political, ecclesiastical, and domestic—that surpasses anything in Paul's own letters. These later writers did not share Paul's sense of the imminent close of history. They were reckoning with an indefinite delay in Christ's return and were concerned to help the church and individual Christians settle down in society. It is perhaps to be expected, given the social, political, and ecclesiastical pressures they experienced, that their initial impulses would be conservative. They were third-generation Christians. The pioneers in the faith were gone. They sought to secure and affirm their communal identity by regrouping around the traditions they had received. They had to think hard about the meaning of those traditions for life in a world that did not seem to be "passing away" very quickly. Perhaps they may be pardoned if they did not always clearly perceive the distinction between accommodation to the realities of the world and capitulation to its values and claims. The church can gratefully receive these later writings as an important part of its Christian heritage; but their teachings should not be confused with those of the apostle, whose moral instruction these later authors sought to adapt and apply for their own situations.

1 Corinthians 14:34-35

In chapters 11–14 of 1 Corinthians, Paul is instructing his congregation to maintain order in worship. Beginning in chapter 12, the matter of spiritual gifts is of special concern because of a dispute in the Corinthian congregation about speaking in tongues, an ecstatic utterance that is unintelligible to others. Paul's overall conclusion is that the gift of ecstatic utterance is permissible but less edifying to the church than the gift of prophesying, which others can understand (see, for instance, 14:39). Moreover, he cautions that where speaking in tongues does take place, it must proceed in orderly fashion and always with an interpreter (14:27-28). Like all else in the Christian community, this "should be done decently and in order" (14:40). So far, so good. But embedded in this discussion there is also a directive that women should remain silent in church (vv. 34-35). This injunction stands within several verses that the NRSV has placed in parentheses and printed as a separate paragraph:

> (As in all the churches of the saints, women should be silent in the churches. For they are not permitted to speak, but should be subordinate, as the law also says. If there is anything they desire to know, let them ask their husbands at home. For it is shameful for a woman to speak in church. Or did the word of God originate with you? Or are you the only ones it has reached?) (vv. 33b-36)

The translators of the NRSV appear to agree with the view, held by many scholars, that verses 33b-36 are not to be attributed to Paul himself. There is, indeed, very strong evidence that at least verses 34-35 should be regarded as a later, non-Pauline addition ("interpolation") to 1 Corinthians. Several kinds of evidence converge to support this conclusion.

1. In one group of ancient manuscripts, verses 34-35 appear after 1 Cor 14:40, concluding the chapter, rather than between verses 33 and 36. In cases of this sort (of which there are other New Testament examples) one has to reckon with the possibility that the "floating" words originated as some ancient reader's marginal comment. Then later scribes, supposing

the words had originally been in the body of the text, "restored" them where they happened to see fit (some locating them after v. 33, others after v. 40).

2. Whether the directive in verses 34-35 is read between verse 33a and verse 37 or after verse 40, it disrupts the literary flow of the passage. (Some interpreters believe this holds true for the whole of vv. 33b-36.) For example, after the reference in verse 33b to "all the churches of the saints," a second reference to "the churches" in verse 34 seems redundant. If, however, verse 33b is attached to what precedes (which both the grammar and the manuscript evidence allow) and verses 34-35 are removed as a later addition, we are left with a good transition:

> And the spirits of prophets are subject to the prophets, for God is a God not of disorder but of peace, as in all the churches of the saints. Or did the word of God originate with *you*? Or are *you* the only ones it has reached? (italics added)

3. Except for the rule that women should be silent in church, the subject of 1 Cor 14:26-40 is the relative merit of prophesying and speaking in tongues, and how these gifts are to be exercised when the congregation is assembled for worship. In discussing these matters, Paul drops not even the slightest hint that the gifts of prophecy and ecstatic utterance are bestowed only on male believers. To be sure, he does direct that when one person is prophesying, others with the gift of prophecy (whether men or women) should remain silent and wait for their turn. And he does direct that those who have the gift of ecstatic utterance (whether men or women) should not exercise it unless there is someone present to interpret. But these are conditional directives, not absolute commands to be silent. It is otherwise in verses 34-35: in church, women are to be silent—period.

4. A further reason for questioning whether the instruction in verses 34-35 originated with Paul is the presence of several un-Pauline features. This is the only place in the certainly Pauline letters where the apostle appeals to the Jewish law ("as the law also says") without in some way indicating where or how the law supports his teaching. Further, the verb translated as "let them ask" appears elsewhere in Paul's letters only in a quotation from the Greek Old Testament (Rom 10:20); and in the only other occurrence of the verb translated "permit," the reference is not, as here, to permission denied ("they are not permitted to speak") but to permission that Paul hopes the Lord will grant (1 Cor 16:7).

5. It is extremely difficult to reconcile the call for women to remain silent in church with Paul's references to women elsewhere in 1 Corinthians. For example, what the apostle says in chapter 7 about the mutual responsibilities of husbands and wives suggests that he judged wives to be fully as capable as husbands in identifying and fulfilling those responsibilities. Above all, the concern he expresses in 11:3-16 (discussed in detail below) about how the Corinthian congregation worships is not that women are among those who pray and prophesy, but only that they do so without the proper head coverings (or hairstyles). Moreover, whereas Paul offers several theological and christological reasons for the views he expresses in chapter 11, the directive in 14:34-35 is supported with only general references to "the law" and what is "shameful."

6. Finally, Paul's concluding statement about the conduct of worship (vv. 37-40) is formulated without any reference to the rule contained in verses 34-35. He summarily commends prophesying, expresses his willingness to allow ecstatic utterance, and states that "all things should be done decently and in order." There is not a word about the need for women to remain silent.

We therefore have substantial evidence that the unqualified instruction about women needing to "be silent in the churches" and "subordinate" to their husbands should not be attributed to the apostle himself. This directive likely originated years later as a marginal comment either by the author of the Pastoral Epistles or by someone who agreed with that author's rule about women: "Let a woman learn in silence with full submission. I permit no woman to teach or to have authority over a man; she is to keep silent" (1 Tim 2:11-12). Indirectly, of course, the marginal comment in 1 Cor 14 and the restrictions placed on women in 1 Timothy provide evidence that a significant number of women *were* fulfilling important responsibilities in the congregations of Paul's founding. Why else would later writers have thought it necessary to issue these and similar rules, and to do so in Paul's name (see also, e.g., Eph 5:22-24; Col 3:18; Titus 2:3-5)?

We are not confined, however, to drawing inferences about the role of women in the congregations of Paul's founding. The apostle's letters offer clear and direct evidence that there were a number of women who played important roles in the conduct of his mission and the leadership of his congregations.

Galatians 3:27-28; 1 Corinthians 12:13

In seeking to understand Paul's view of the status and role of women in the church, we do well to begin with the important declaration that he addressed to the Galatians (3:27-28): "As many of you as were baptized into Christ have clothed yourselves with Christ. There is no longer Jew or Greek, there is no longer slave or free, there is no longer male and female; for all of you are one in Christ Jesus."

Most interpreters believe that Paul is quoting here from a baptismal liturgy that was used in his and other Christian congregations, and that is echoed as well in Rom 10:12; 1 Cor 12:13; and Col 3:11. Within its original liturgical setting, it was addressed to newly baptized persons, declaring them to have been transferred into a believing community that participates in a wholly new order of existence. They now inhabit a realm in which their lives are no longer defined by the religious, social, and gender distinctions they had previously taken for granted as "the way the world works."

In quoting this baptismal declaration, Paul has adhered closely to its probably original threefold reference to Jews/Greeks, slaves/free, and male/female. Although he quotes the entire statement, only the first of the three pairs impinges directly on the main issue addressed in Galatians: What should be required of Gentiles who accept the gospel? Must they obey the law of Moses as most Jewish converts were continuing to do? In other words, must Gentiles become good Jews in order to be good Christians? Paul has invoked the baptismal formula as part of his answer: everyone who is "baptized into Christ," whether a Jew or a Gentile, has experienced a new creation and been granted a new identity. Now they are "clothed . . . with Christ," and it is no longer their cultural or religious heritage that defines who they are, for "there is no longer Jew or Greek." As one interpreter puts it, the "differences that earlier might have separated them have now disappeared because everyone looks like Christ!" (S. K. Williams). Paul therefore rejects the claim that the Jewish law must be imposed on Gentile believers. It is through incorporation in Christ, not through the law, that the believing community finds its identity and integrity. Using the first-person singular for emphasis, the apostle speaks of this new community as a whole when he says, "Through the law I died to the law, so that I might live to God. I have been crucified with Christ; and it is no longer I who live, but it is Christ who lives in me. And the life I now live in the flesh I live by faith in the Son of God, who loved me and gave himself for me" (Gal 2:19-20).

Paul recognized that what baptism into Christ does to cultural, religious, and ethnic distinctions, it also does to social and gender distinctions. In Christ, these, too, have been relativized, even though they may remain. He also recognized, of course, that one's social position may change. In Roman times, for instance, being a "slave" or "free" was not necessarily a permanent condition. In 1 Cor 7:21 he counsels slaves to gain their freedom if possible (the NRSV alternative translation is to be accepted), and in his letter to Philemon he seems to be appealing for the emancipation of the slave Onesimus. Nonetheless, even if Onesimus remains a slave, "in Christ" that social position is of no more ultimate consequence than his being a male and (probably) a Gentile.

Sharp-eyed readers will notice that the statement "there is no longer male and female" departs from the form of the two preceding clauses, which read: "there is no longer x *or* y." The variation, "male *and* female," which conveys the same meaning, reflects the wording of the statement in Gen 1:27 that "God created humankind . . . *male and female*" (italics added). This echo of Gen 1 calls attention to how radically the new order of existence established in Christ has been conceived: even the differentiation of "male and female" ordained by God at the original creation has been set aside.

The same baptismal affirmation is reflected in 1 Cor 12:13 as Paul begins to develop his image of the church as the "body of Christ" (12:12-27). This passage provides us a closer look at what he understands the traditional statement to mean. It means that those who are baptized into Christ, although they have different gifts, are one in Christ and bound together in their dependence on the same God (vv. 4-11). It means that although they serve in diverse ways, all "have the same care for one another" (v. 25). It means that they are no longer beholden to society's notions of who are to be esteemed as "honorable" and who are to be dismissed as unpresentable; the apostle urges the Corinthians to regard each and every member of Christ's body as not only "respectable" but "indispensable" (vv. 22-24).

We must also reckon, however, with Paul's having omitted one part of the baptismal declaration when he cites it at the beginning of this passage (1 Cor 12:13): "For in the one Spirit we were all baptized into one body—Jews or Greeks, slaves or free—and we were all made to drink of one Spirit." The absence of the third clause, "male and female," is surely not due to simple oversight or to Paul's unwillingness to recognize the full partnership of men and women in the body of Christ. He probably omitted the clause because of what he knew about the state of affairs in the Corinthian congregation. In chapter 2 we saw that certain Corinthian Christians believed that those who claim to belong to Christ should abstain from sex even within marriage. It is very likely that some of them supported this view by appealing to the baptismal declaration that "there is no longer male and female." Since we know that the apostle himself did not interpret the statement as supporting any such conclusion, it is understandable that he would choose to omit it from the formula as he cites it for this congregation. The omission of the third clause should, therefore, not be taken as evidence that Paul harbored doubts about there being "no longer male and female." It is evidence, rather, that he took that declaration seriously and wanted to prevent its misuse.

1 Corinthians 11:2-16

How fully did Paul appreciate and embrace the *practical implications* of the male/female clause in the baptismal affirmation? Some interpreters cite 1 Cor 11:2-16 as an indication that he continued to hold certain conventional, patriarchal views of women. Attempts to show that this passage, like 1 Cor 14:34-35, is a later, non-Pauline addition to the letter have been generally rejected for lack of evidence. We are left, then, with several statements that, at first glance, appear to reflect a view of women that is at odds with the baptismal affirmation.

I want you to understand that Christ is the head of every man, and the husband is the head of his wife, and God is the head of Christ. . . . A man . . . is the image and reflection of God; but woman is the reflection of man. Indeed, man was not made from woman, but woman from man. Neither was man created for the sake of woman, but woman for the sake of man. (1 Cor 11:3, 7-9)

In addition, the seemingly patriarchal aspect of these comments has tended to influence the translation of verse 10. The rather cryptic Greek text—"the woman ought to have authority on the head"—is often interpreted to mean that a woman "ought to wear upon her head something to symbolize her subjection" (E. J. Goodspeed's translation; see also the JB and the NAB, 1970). And some such interpretation is allowed even by more ambiguous renderings like that of the NRSV, "a woman ought to have a symbol of authority on her head" (see also the ASV, the NIV, and the NAB, 1986).

First impressions can mislead, however, especially in this case where Paul's reasoning is not easy to follow. We can best work through this logical thicket if we start by determining what the Apostle is asking of whom. This will put us in a better position to consider the supporting arguments he offers, and whether they are in violation of the principle, "no longer male and female."

The Aim of the Passage

Paul's specific concern is succinctly expressed in verse 13: "Judge for yourselves: is it proper for a woman to pray to God with her head unveiled?" Nothing indicates that the Corinthian Christians had raised this question with Paul. He seems to have heard in some roundabout way that certain women of the congregation were praying (and prophesying, see v. 5) with their heads uncovered—or perhaps with their hair unbound and loose. Whether the concern is with head coverings or hairstyles (the translation of several terms is in dispute), the main point is clear: the apostle disapproves of how these Corinthian women appear when they pray and prophesy. While it is proper, he says, for the men to pray and prophesy with uncovered heads, it is not proper for the women to do so. His judgment about this is in accord with the conventional view in his day, that modesty requires a woman to cover her head (or bind up her loose hair) when she is out in public.

Considering how Paul opens the discussion—"I want you to understand" (v. 3)—and the number of arguments he offers to support his instruction, this is probably the first time he has conveyed his views on the subject to the Corinthian church. The practice of women praying and prophesying with uncovered heads had evidently developed since his departure. It may well have been prompted by the Corinthians' overemphasis on the present manifestations of salvation, combined with their interpretation of "no longer male and female" as requiring the *elimination* of all sexual distinctions. In any case, it is clear that Paul's aim in this passage is to direct that women continue to be attired as women when they pray or prophesy in church.

But no less clear than Paul's specific aim is what he takes for granted: it is perfectly right and proper for women to offer prayers and prophecies when the church is assembled for worship. His direction is not that women cease from praying and prophesying, but that they do so with their heads covered, *as women*. This does not, however, change the fact that *functionally* their participation in worship is no different from that of men.

Paul's Reasoning

The topic of this passage does not surface until verses 4-6. To encourage their openness to what will follow, Paul starts out by complimenting the Corinthians for keeping "the traditions" that he had handed on to them, presumably at the time of their conversion (v. 2). His statement of intention in verse 3 moves closer to the topic by introducing the key term *head*: "But I want you to understand that Christ is the head of every man, and the husband is the head of his wife, and God is the head of Christ." The words rendered in this NRSV translation as "the husband . . . his wife" can also be translated as "the man . . . a woman," and they probably should be, since Paul has in mind the creation of the first "man" and first "woman" (vv. 8-9).

It would be reasonable to expect Paul to follow up the statement in verse 3 with a rule like the one in 1 Cor 14:34-35, that women should remain silent in church and be subordinate to their husbands. For even if "head" is intended as a metaphor for "source," the allusion being to woman's creation from man (see v. 8 and Gen 2:18-23), this could still be read as implying man's superiority. The apostle does not, however, draw that conclusion. Abruptly leaving the metaphor behind, in the rest of this passage he uses "head" only in a literal sense. His conclusion is not that the Corinthian women should be silent and subordinate, but that they should keep their heads covered (or hair arranged) as women customarily do (vv. 4-6). It is the *distinctiveness* of women and men, respectively, not the subordination of women to men, that Paul seems to believe the statement in verse 3 somehow supports.

The distinctiveness of the sexes is still in view in verses 7-9, where the Apostle draws on Gen 1–2 to show that God *created* male and female to be different. He alludes, first, to Gen 1:26-28, according to which "God created humankind in his image, in the image of God he created them; male and female he created them" (v. 27). Passing over the statement that humankind as a whole bears God's image, Paul focuses on God's differentiation of male and female. He introduces a term not present in Genesis ("glory") when he says that man is "the image and glory of God;

but woman is the glory of man" (v. 7 NRSV alternative translation). This claim is supported with the reminder that "man was not made from woman, but woman from man. Neither was man created for the sake of woman, but woman for the sake of man" (vv. 8-9, alluding to Gen 2:18-23). He is apparently reasoning that because the man was created by and for God, he manifests God's splendor, while the woman manifests the man's splendor (which is God's splendor at second remove) because she was created from him to be his companion. Thus, through the circumstances of creation, woman is different from man.

The outcome of the apostle's reading of Gen 1–2 is presented in verse 10, which says nothing about the subordination of women to men. To the contrary, Paul infers from Scripture that women who pray or prophesy in church should cover their heads to show their *authority* (v. 10): "And so, because of this, and also because of the angels, a woman ought to wear something on her head, as a sign of her authority" (CEV; cf. REB: "and therefore a woman must have the sign of her authority on her head, out of regard for the angels"). Paul's reference to "angels" remains enigmatic, despite many scholarly attempts to explain it. It is also unclear why he regarded a woman's head covering as signifying her authority. Did he suppose—to mention just one possibility—that it freed her from the limitation of reflecting the "glory" of man so that she could pray and prophesy to the glory of God? Here again, the apostle's thinking eludes us. Respecting the critical matter, however, we can be confident: the instruction about head coverings was not given to curtail the participation of women in the church; its effect was to *affirm* their authority to pray and prophesy during the congregation's worship.

Those who struggle to follow the twists and turns of Paul's reasoning on this topic can take some comfort in the fact that even he seems to have worried about being misunderstood. Immediately after deploying the creation accounts to make his case, he interrupts his argument with a striking correction of it: "Nevertheless, in the Lord woman is not independent of man or man independent of woman. For just as woman came from man, so man comes through woman; but all things come from God" (vv. 11-12).

It is not difficult to hear in these words an echo of the traditional baptismal affirmation that there is "no longer male and female." With the phrase "in the Lord," Paul directs attention to the *new* creation, where hierarchical judgments about "inferior" and "superior" have no place. Alluding once more to the original creation, Paul explains that even though woman had in the beginning been made from man, ever since then man has been born from woman (through the procreative process of childbirth); so, indeed, neither can exist without the other. His most fundamental claim, however, is that "all things come from God." For Paul, this defines who people are—not their ethnic or religious heritage, social position, or sexual status, but their common dependence upon the one God by whom they have been graced with life.

Perhaps sensing that his statements in verses 11-12 could potentially undermine his whole argument up to this point, Paul offers one last reason why women should cover their heads (vv. 13-15). "Nature itself," he claims, teaches that it is "proper" for a woman to wear her hair long and bound up as a covering for her head (or bound up in a way that allows for a head covering). As used here, "nature" does not refer to *creation* (Paul's argument from creation concluded with v. 10) or to the supposed properties of the physical world. It refers, rather, to *social convention,* to the culture's established beliefs about "the way things are" and therefore ought to be. The grammatically fractured sentence that follows (v. 16) is less a part of the argument than a way of closing it down: "But if anyone is disposed to be contentious—we have no such custom, nor do the churches of God" (v. 16). In the end, Paul has no way of enforcing the practice he commends (the "if" clause of his conditional sentence is left dangling without a "then" clause). He can only warn the Corinthians that if they dispute his reasoning and persist with their present practice, they will be departing from the practice that obtains in his other congregations.

Finally, then, we must acknowledge that certain aspects of Paul's argument for women's head coverings (vv. 3-10) remain unclear. And also, that he comes very close to undermining it with the qualification, "Nevertheless, in the Lord woman is not independent of man or man independent of woman," and "all things come from God" (vv. 11-12). At the same time, however, this all-important "nevertheless" statement confirms what a patient reading of the entire passage discloses. The Apostle's directive about head coverings both presumes and supports the authority of women to pray and prophesy in church, and is consistent with his commitment to the baptismal declaration that "there is no longer male and female."

But what about Paul's *own* dealings with women? Did he, in fact, practice what he preached?

Women in Paul's Ministry

We know next to nothing about the women in Paul's family. There is a brief remark in the book of Acts that "the son of Paul's sister" warned him of an assassination plot (23:16). This unnamed sister is mentioned nowhere else, however, and there is no reference at all to their mother. If Paul was ever married, the marriage probably ended before or shortly after his conversion, and certainly before the writing of 1 Corinthians (see 1 Cor 7:7; 9:5). We therefore know nothing about his family life that could help us assess his relationships with or attitudes toward women. We do, however, know a good deal about Paul's dealings with women in the church; more than a dozen women are named or otherwise identified in his letters. The picture that emerges is of an apostle who in practice as well as in principle supports the view that in Christ Jesus "there is no longer male and female."

Prisca (Priscilla)

One of Paul's closest associates in ministry was Prisca, a woman mentioned in two of his letters and also in the book of Acts, where she is called Priscilla (the diminutive, familiar form of her name). She may have belonged to a wealthy Roman family of high social status. Her husband, Aquila, identified in Acts as "a native of Pontus" (18:2), may have been a freeborn Jew. According to Acts, this couple had for a while resided in the imperial capital but then fled to Corinth when Emperor Claudius, probably in the year 49, "ordered all Jews to leave Rome" (18:2). This was during a period when, according to other ancient sources, the Jewish community in Rome was in turmoil because there were some Jews who had come to believe in Christ. Acts exaggerates when it reports that "all Jews" were expelled by Claudius, but the leading agitators undoubtedly were; and certain other Jews, including Jewish Christians, may well have fled the city at the same time.

Whether Prisca and Aquila were already Christians when they arrived in Corinth, or whether they were converted there, perhaps by Paul himself, we do not know. That they did meet Paul in Corinth is clear (Acts 18:1-2), and they may have been associated with him in the "same trade," as Acts also reports (18:3). We are told, further, that this couple accompanied Paul when he went on to Ephesus but that they did not accompany him when he took a ship from there for Caesarea (Acts 18:18-19).

The residence of Prisca and Aquila in Ephesus is confirmed when Paul, writing from that city, conveys their greetings to the church in Corinth: "Aquila and Prisca, together with the church in their house, greet you warmly in the Lord" (1 Cor 16:19). The reference to "their house" sounds natural enough to us, but it would have sounded far less so to the members of Paul's Corinthian congregation. Because both law and custom assigned to the male special rights and duties as the head of the household, one would have expected, rather, a reference to "the church in Aquila's house." Paul's choice, instead, of the plural, "their," suggests that he viewed Prisca as a full partner with Aquila both in their marriage and in sponsoring a house church. Significantly, neither Paul nor the author of Acts ever refers to "Aquila and his wife"—or, for that matter, to "Prisca and her husband."

Paul's other reference to this couple occurs near the close of his letter to the Romans, written several years after 1 Corinthians, in 56 or 57. By this time, Prisca and Aquila have left Ephesus and made their way back to Rome. Paul, who is once more in Corinth, now conveys greetings *to* them (Rom 16:3-5a): "Greet Prisca and Aquila, who work with me in Christ Jesus, and who risked their necks for my life, to whom not only I give thanks, but also all the churches of the Gentiles. Greet also the church in their house."

There is much to notice in just these few lines.

1. Paul refers again to "*their* house," and he now mentions Prisca's name ahead of her husband's. This sequence (see also Acts 18:18, 26; 2 Tim 4:19) could signal her higher social standing, her greater importance in the leadership of the house church, or both. In any event, Paul certainly does not view her as subordinate to Aquila.

2. The apostle describes both of them as his "co-workers in Christ Jesus" (my translation). This puts Prisca as well as her husband on a par with people like Timothy and Titus (also called "co-workers"; e.g., Rom 16:21; 2 Cor 8:23), to whom Paul assigned weighty and complicated responsibilities.

3. They had "risked their necks" for the apostle's life. Although Paul does not say how, when, or where, we can imagine that they had come to his assistance when all three were resident in Ephesus, where the apostle

faced life-threatening difficulties (1 Cor 15:32; 2 Cor 1:8-9). Whatever the circumstances, their ability to assist Paul, like their travel (from Rome to Corinth to Ephesus, and back to Rome) and their sponsorship of house churches, suggests that they were relatively well off and of relatively high social standing. For these same reasons, they were probably well known, at least by reputation, in many of the Pauline congregations (note "all the churches of the Gentiles," v. 4).

According to Acts, sometime after Paul left Ephesus, the renowned Apollos arrived there. He is identified as a Jewish Christian from Alexandria who was "eloquent" and "well-versed in the scriptures" (Acts 18:24-25). Paul mentions him too and apparently knew him well (1 Cor 1:12; 3:4-5, 22; 4:6; 16:12). Among the Ephesians who heard Apollos were "Priscilla and Aquila," but they seem not to have been satisfied with his preaching of the gospel. So, in the telling of Acts, "they took him aside and explained the Way of God to him more accurately" (18:26). Here we are presented with the remarkable picture of a *woman* (named before her husband) who is engaged in the theological instruction of a reputedly learned preacher of the gospel. She was violating the rule of 1 Tim 2:12, which "permit[s] no woman to teach or to have authority over a man"! To be sure, the author of Luke–Acts, after the fashion of many ancient writers, tended to mold history and traditions in keeping with his own ideas and objectives. In writing of Jesus, for example, he highlighted the importance of the many women who became disciples. Nevertheless, his portrayal of Prisca/Priscilla is entirely consistent with what we know about her importance from the more historically secure comments in Paul's letters.

Phoebe

Another woman who was closely associated with Paul's ministry is known to us from his letter to the Romans (16:1-2): "I commend to you our sister Phoebe, a deacon of the church at Cenchreae, so that you may welcome her in the Lord as is fitting for the saints, and help her in whatever she may require from you, for she has been a benefactor of many and of myself as well."

Although an older theory held that chapter 16 of Romans originated as a note to the church in Ephesus, it is now generally agreed that at least the first sixteen verses have always been part of this letter. It is rather surprising that the woman Paul commends in the first two verses is known to us only from this passage because she must have come to be widely known in Pauline circles. The reference to her as "our sister" identifies her as a fellow believer, and the name "Phoebe" indicates that she was probably a Gentile Christian. According to Paul, she served in two specific capacities.

First, she was "a deacon of the church at Cenchreae." Cenchreae was one of the port cities of Corinth, just a few miles distant. Translations that persist in calling Phoebe a "deaconess" are misleading, for Paul uses the masculine form, "deacon"; the feminine form was not in use until several centuries later. Nothing suggests that Phoebe belonged to some special order of female deacons ("deaconesses") of lesser importance than male deacons. To be a "deacon," male or female, was to be engaged in *serving others*, for which the Greek word is *diakonia* (often translated as "ministry" in the NRSV). There were various kinds of services to be performed within the Christian communities of Paul's day, and he recognizes this when he lists "varieties of services" as one of the gifts of the Spirit (1 Cor 12:5). When Paul calls Phoebe a "deacon," he is putting her on a par with all other servants of Christ, including himself, Apollos, and Timothy (e.g., 1 Cor 3:5-6; Phil 1:1).

Second, Paul says that she was "a benefactor of many and of myself as well." The literal meaning of the Greek word that the NRSV translates as "benefactor" is *one who stands before*, and in ancient Greek texts it was often used of a presiding officer. But it was also used of a person who supported a religious or other association as its *patron*. In an inscription pertaining to one specific Hellenistic religious society, the word stands first in a list of the group's officers, the others being chief priest, scribe, custodians, and trustees. Thus, even if there were several deacons in the church in Cenchreae (as there were in the Philippian church, Phil 1:1), Phoebe's role as its "benefactor" was of critical importance. She must have had substantial financial resources and was doubtless a person of high social standing. Indeed, Paul acknowledges that he himself had benefited from her support. Given the strictly ordered patron-client structure of Greco-Roman society, he is implicitly presenting himself, in this respect, as inferior to and dependent upon her.

Yet Paul never endorsed terms like *superior* and *inferior* for use within the church. However great the disparity between his and Phoebe's material wealth and social status, she was first and foremost his "sister" in Christ. Moreover, in his role as apostle *he* is the one who commends *her* to the congregations in Rome. She was evidently the bearer of his letter to those congregations, and as such she would have been the one responsible for interpreting and clarifying it for them. We can only speculate about what Paul had in mind when he requested that they "help her in whatever she may require" from them. As a person of means and standing, she would not have required their help in meeting her personal needs. One plausible suggestion is that Paul had charged her with enlisting support for his projected mission to Spain, which he was planning to launch from Rome (15:22-28).

Euodia and Syntyche

The church at Philippi had been founded by Paul, and his subsequent relationship to the Philippian congregation remained warm and cordial. According to Acts, he had preached first to some women of the city. He baptized one of them, Lydia, and she provided food and shelter for the apostle and his companions (16:11-15). The same narrative goes on to say that after Paul and Silas were miraculously released from jail, the apostle made it a point to visit Lydia before leaving the city (Acts 16:40). Yet he himself never mentions this woman, and as so often in Acts, the story leaves us wondering about the reliability of the information.

Two other Philippian women are, however, mentioned by Paul himself. In a letter to the church in Philippi he writes,

> I urge Euodia and I urge Syntyche to be of the same mind in the Lord. Yes, and I ask you also, my loyal companion, help these women, for they have struggled beside me in the work of the gospel, together with Clement and the rest of my co-workers, whose names are in the book of life. (4:2-3)

The names indicate that Euodia and Syntyche were Gentile Christians, and it is evident that they were either members of the Philippian congregation or closely associated with it in some other way. It is unlikely, although not impossible, that one or both were among the "bishops" or "deacons" mentioned in Phil 1:1. Somehow the relationship between them had become strained, yet Paul provides no details; the congregation itself was presumably well aware of the circumstances.

The disagreement between Euodia and Syntyche was of enough consequence that the apostle gives it his specific attention. This was not just a case of two "bickering women." There is, in fact, no other instance where Paul singles out by name people in his congregations who need to be called to account. We note, as well, that he appeals to them individually: "I urge Euodia and I urge Syntyche." Beyond this, he requests a third party—some unnamed "loyal companion" of his—to step in and help settle the dispute. All of this suggests that these two women had significant responsibilities in the Christian community of Philippi.

The importance of Euodia and Syntyche is confirmed when Paul credits them with having "struggled beside [him] in the work of the gospel," and associates them closely "with Clement and the rest of my coworkers." (Clement is mentioned nowhere else in Paul's letters or the book of Acts.) Customarily, Paul used expressions like "the work of the gospel" with reference to the missionary preaching and labors in which he and various associates were engaged (e.g., Rom 1:9; 2 Cor 10:14; 1 Thess 3:2). It is possible, therefore, that Euodia and Syntyche had been associated with Paul in places beyond Philippi. In addition, his comment that they had "struggled" beside him opens the possibility that they had shared with him in suffering for the gospel (see Phil 1:27-28).

Chloe

Paul's opening appeal in 1 Corinthians is for unity in a congregation that is, reportedly, full of dissension and quarreling (1:10). Information about these difficulties had come to him in Ephesus, the city from which he was writing (see 16:8), and he identifies his informants as "Chloe's people" (1:11)—literally, "those who belong to Chloe." The name itself tells us that Chloe was a woman, and the fact that Paul identifies her only by name suggests that she was someone already well known to the Corinthians and respected by them. It is inherently more probable that she was a Christian than that she was not, and that she and her "people" were residents of Ephesus rather than Corinth. Her "people" could have been family members, friends, business associates, or slaves; and since it is she who is named, their travel to and from Corinth was likely on her behalf. It would therefore appear that Chloe, like Phoebe of Cenchreae, was a woman with significant material resources and of relatively high social status. We do not know, however, to what extent she may have supported the Ephesian church or Paul's ministry.

Apphia

Although Philemon (probably a resident of Colossae) is the primary addressee of the letter that is known by his name, Paul addressed the letter, as well, to "Apphia our sister, to Archippus our fellow soldier, and to the church in your house" (Phlm 1b-2). In the final phrase, "your" is singular and probably refers to Philemon, the person named first. It is possible, but unlikely, that Apphia was Philemon's wife and thus cohost of the church. Paul addresses her as "the sister" (NRSV alternative translation), which suggests that she had standing in her own right as one of the leaders of this Christian community (and the same holds for Archippus, identified as "our fellow soldier"). What Apphia's special responsibilities may have been, we do not know, but they were no doubt significant. Indeed, it is possible that Apphia and Archippus are included as addressees because Paul believed they could be influential in persuading Philemon to heed his appeals on behalf of this man's slave Onesimus.

Junia

Junia is one of a number of people to whom Paul sends greetings at the end of Romans (16:7): "Greet Andronicus and Junia, my relatives who were in prison with me; they are prominent among the apostles, and they were in Christ before I was." There has been a long tradition of reading the second of these names as if it were that of a male, despite clear linguistic and textual evidence that it is a woman's name. The traditional interpretation has no other basis than the unfounded presumption of male commentators that a woman could not possibly have been an apostle, let alone "prominent" within the apostolic circle. Although this tradition persists in some widely used English translations (e.g., "Junias" in the NJB and the NIV), scholarship has shown definitively that Paul was referring to a woman; and also that he was identifying her, along with

Andronicus, as "prominent among the apostles" (not "regarded as prominent *by* the apostles").

Neither Andronicus nor Junia is named elsewhere in the New Testament, so we know nothing more about them than what Paul says here. When he calls them his "kinfolk" (NRSV: "relatives"), he probably means that, like himself, they were ethnic Jews (this is how he had used the same word in Rom 9:3). And like "Prisca and Aquila" (v. 3), "Andronicus and Junia" were probably husband and wife. Several other facts about this couple are especially noteworthy.

1. They had committed themselves to the gospel even before Paul had received his call to apostleship ("they were in Christ before I was"). Since Paul, by the time of this letter, had probably been an apostle for more than twenty years, Andronicus and Junia were longtime believers, likely well and widely known in Christian circles.

2. They were "prominent among the apostles." When Paul spoke of apostles (whom he thought of as exercising a spiritual gift, 1 Cor 12:28), he meant itinerant missionaries who were engaged in preaching the gospel and founding churches. We do not know when or where Andronicus and Junia had begun their apostolic work or what had brought them to Rome. We also do not know whether Paul described them as "prominent" because they had been active for so long in the service of the gospel or for some other reason. About one important point, however, there is no doubt: "prominent among the apostles" applies no less to Junia than to Andronicus. That is, Junia did not just *accompany* her husband, as may have been the case with "the other apostles and the brothers of the Lord and Cephas" (1 Cor 9:5). She was in her own right a full-fledged and prominent preacher of the gospel.

3. On at least one occasion Andronicus and Junia had been imprisoned—we may presume, for their preaching of the gospel. The NRSV translators interpret Paul as saying that they had been imprisoned *with*

him somewhere, and this is quite possible. But his words could also be translated to mean that they, *like* himself, had been imprisoned in one or more places. Perhaps their prominence as apostles derived at least in part from their imprisonment and the circumstances that led to it.

Some Other Women in Rome

At the close of his letter to the Roman Christians, Paul sends greetings to several women in addition to Prisca and Junia. Among them are Mary (16:6), Tryphaena, Tryphosa, and Persis (v. 12). Choosing a term that he often used of his own apostolic labors (e.g., 1 Cor 15:10), he identifies each of them as having "worked" for the Lord. Three additional women to whom he sends greetings are the unnamed mother of Rufus (v. 13), a woman by the name of Julia, and the unnamed sister of Nereus (v. 15). Julia and Nereus's sister are otherwise unidentified and unknown, although it has been speculated that Julia was the wife of Philologus, whose name immediately precedes hers, and that Nereus and his sister were their children. When the apostle calls the mother of Rufus "a mother to me also" (v. 13), that is only enough to make us wish that he would have said more. There is the intriguing possibility, quite unprovable, that she was the wife of Simon of Cyrene, who reportedly helped Jesus carry his cross and was the father of two sons, Alexander and Rufus (Mark 15:21). But that possible connection aside, what was her tie to Paul? Where had their paths crossed (he had not yet been to Rome)? Had he been a regular guest in her home? Had she, like Phoebe, been one of his benefactors? Although these questions remain unanswered, there is no question that Paul was eager to acknowledge his indebtedness to her.

Observations and Reflections

We have seen that it is important, particularly on the subject of women in the church, to distinguish between the apostle's own letters and those written in his name after his death. This is not to say that the views and practices of those who came after Paul may be ignored. After all, Ephesians, Colossians, and the Pastoral Epistles are also part of the church's canon of Scripture. Moreover, each of these writings, like each of Paul's own letters, deserves to be interpreted in the light of its particular social, historical, and religious context. The present chapter, however, in keeping with the aim of this book, has focused exclusively on the apostle's own view of women in the church. The results are clear.

1. *In accord with the baptismal declaration that he cites to the Galatians, Paul affirmed that in Christ Jesus "there is no longer male and female."* He called on believers to embrace the radically new order of existence that he understood God to have established in Christ, knowing that their common dependence on God's grace and incorporation into Christ had also brought them into a new relationship with one another. Paul recognized that religious, ethnic, social, and sexual distinctions remained, but he did not regard them as constituting one's true identity. [Although believers are still either Jew or Greek, slave or free, male or female, their existence has been radically qualified and transformed by the new, definitive reality of their being "in Christ."]

2. *Nothing in Paul's concrete teaching on matters pertaining to women is incompatible with his belief that "there is no longer male and female."* The main passage that has to be tested in this connection is 1 Cor 11:2-16, since it is often used in support of the view that women are to remain subordinate in all ways to men. We have seen, however, that one must consider the situation Paul was addressing in that passage and avoid applying his arguments to matters for which they were not formulated. When his own intentions there are honored, and when his own words about the interdependence of man and woman are heeded, one sees that his instruction not only accommodates but supports the baptismal declaration.

3. *There is ample evidence that women were among Paul's closest missionary associates and among the most prominent leaders in his churches.* Moreover, we never find him distinguishing the spiritual gifts or functions or accomplishments of women from those of men. Paraphrasing Paul, one might ask: Must all apostles and prophets be male and Jewish? Must all benefactors be freeborn and Gentile? Must all deacons and teachers be female? Must all helpers be slaves? Paul's response would be unequivocal: Absolutely not! It can be said with some confidence that Paul's practice, no less than his teaching, was consistent with his commitment to the baptismal declaration that "there is no longer Jew or Greek, there is no longer slave or free, there is no longer male and female; for all of you are one in Christ Jesus."

One further observation can underscore what we have discovered about Paul's views and practice concerning women in the church. In three different letters he characterizes his *own* ministry by employing maternal imagery. In 1 Thess 2:7c-8 he portrays himself as a nursing mother: "Having as much affection for you as a nurse who tenderly cares for her own children, we are determined to share with you not only the gospel of God but also our own selves, because you have become very dear to us" (my translation). He presents himself similarly in 1 Cor 3:1-3a. When the Corinthians were still "infants in Christ," he fed them only with milk because they were not ready for "solid food." And in Gal 4:19 he speaks as a worried mother, addressing his Galatian converts as his "little children" for whom he is reliving "the pain of childbirth" until they allow Christ to be "formed" in them. We can take Paul's use of this imagery as further evidence—indirect, but no less telling—that he welcomed women as full-fledged partners in his mission and leaders in his congregations.

For Further Reading

Statements cited in this chapter that oppose the ordination of women: Pope John Paul II, *Ordinatio Sacerdotalis* (see www.vatican.va/holy_

father/john_paul_ii); Article 6 of "The Baptist Faith and Message," adopted by the Southern Baptist Convention (June 14, 2000; see www.sbc.net/bfm); R. Albert Mohler, "The Feminization of the Ministry—A Milestone in Britain" (November 14, 2007; see www.albert mohler.com). The statement made in the meeting of a Dallas congregation is cited from an unpublished paper provided by its author to the woman who was seeking to be ordained.

Citations in this chapter from ancient sources: the *Testament of Reuben* and the *Letter of Aristeas* are cited from the translations in James H. Charlesworth, ed., *The Old Testament Pseudepigrapha* (2 vols.; Garden City, N.Y.: Doubleday, 1983); Epictetus, Philo, and Plutarch are cited from the translations in the Loeb Classical Library (Cambridge, Mass.: Harvard University Press, various years). For other ancient sources documenting the life and circumstances of women in the Greco-Roman world, see Mary R. Lefkowitz and Maureen B. Fant, *Women's Life in Greece and Rome: A Sourcebook in Translation* (3rd ed.; Baltimore: Johns Hopkins University Press, 2005).

There are important discussions of Gal 3:28 and 1 Cor 11:2-16 in a classic study by Elisabeth Schüssler Fiorenza, *In Memory of Her: A Feminist Theological Reconstruction of Christian Origins* (10th anniversary ed.; New York: Crossroad, 1994). For these and the other New Testament passages discussed in this chapter, see also Carol A. Newsom and Sharon H. Ringe, eds., *The Women's Bible Commentary: Expanded Edition* (Louisville: Westminster John Knox, 1998). Paul's use of maternal imagery is examined in detail by Beverly Roberts Gaventa, *Our Mother Saint Paul* (Louisville and London: Westminster John Knox, 2007).

Commentaries on Romans are listed with the "Further Reading" at the end of chapter 3. For the evidence in favor of reading the disputed name in Rom 16:7 as "Junia," and for counting her "among the apostles," see Eldon Jay Epp, *Junia: The First Woman Apostle* (Minneapolis: Fortress, 2005).

Commentaries on 1 Corinthians are listed with the "Further Reading" at the end of chapter 2. The commentary by Gordon Fee presents evidence and arguments for the position adopted in the present book, that 1 Cor 14:34-35 is a later, non-Pauline addition (see also Epp, *Junia*, 15–20). Arguments on the other side of this question are given by L. Ann Jervis, "1 Corinthians 14.34-35: A Reconsideration of Paul's Limitation of the Free Speech of Some Corinthian Women," *Journal for the Study of the New Testament* 58 (1995): 51–74. For a detailed, nuanced study of 1 Cor 11:2-16, see Francis Watson, *Agape, Eros, Gender: Towards a Pauline Sexual Ethic* (Cambridge, U.K.: Cambridge University Press, 2000), 40–89.

Commentaries on Galatians: Beverly R. Gaventa, "Galatians," in *Eerdmans Commentary on the Bible* (ed. J. D. G. Dunn and J. W. Rogerson; Grand Rapids, and Cambridge, U.K.: Eerdmans, 2003), 1374–84; Richard B. Hays, "Galatians: Introduction, Commentary, and Reflections," in *The New Interpreter's Bible* 11 (ed. L. E. Keck et al.; Nashville: Abingdon Press, 2000), 181–348; Sam K. Williams, *Galatians* (Abingdon New Testament Commentaries; Nashville: Abingdon Press, 1997), see 106 for the statement quoted in this chapter. More detailed: J. Louis Martyn, *Galatians: A New Translation with Introduction and Commentary* (Anchor Bible 33A; New York: Doubleday, 1997).

Commentaries on Colossians and Ephesians: David M. Hay, *Colossians* (Abingdon New Testament Commentaries; Nashville: Abingdon Press, 2000); Morna D. Hooker, "Colossians," in *Eerdmans Commentary on the Bible* (ed. J. D. G. Dunn and J. W. Rogerson; Grand Rapids, and Cambridge, U.K.: Eerdmans, 2003), 1404–12; in *The New Interpreter's Bible* 11 (ed. L. E. Keck et al.; Nashville: Abingdon Press, 2000), see Andrew T. Lincoln, "Colossians: Introduction, Commentary, and Reflections," 551–669, and Pheme Perkins, "Ephesians: Introduction, Commentary, and Reflections," 349–466. More detailed: Margaret Y.

MacDonald, *Colossians and Ephesians* (Sacra Pagina; Collegeville, Minn.: Liturgical Press, 2000).

Commentaries on the Pastoral Epistles: Jouette M. Bassler, *1 Timothy, 2 Timothy, Titus* (Abingdon New Testament Commentaries; Nashville: Abingdon Press, 1996); James D. G. Dunn, "Pastoral Epistles: Introduction, Commentary, and Reflections," in *The New Interpreter's Bible* 11 (ed. L. E. Keck et al.; Nashville: Abingdon Press, 2000), 775–880; Pheme Perkins, "Pastoral Epistles," in *Eerdmans Commentary on the Bible* (ed. J. D. G. Dunn and J. W. Rogerson; Grand Rapids, and Cambridge, U.K.: Eerdmans, 2003), 1428–46. More detailed: Raymond F. Collins, *1 & 2 Timothy and Titus: A Commentary* (New Testament Library; Louisville and London: Westminster John Knox, 2002).

CHAPTER 5

THE CHURCH IN THE WORLD

The topics discussed in the preceding chapters have kept our attention fixed largely on questions about the personal conduct of individual believers, their family relationships, and their life within the church. At the same time, however, we have had to take account of the broader historical, cultural, and social contexts within which Paul's moral instructions were given and received. For the challenge facing his converts, both as individual believers and as members of the believing community, was how to remain faithful to the gospel despite the pressures, uncertainties, and risks they faced in an unbelieving society. It is therefore appropriate that we now broaden our inquiry to consider what Paul had to say about the church's relation to the world. Did he call for believers to *reject* society's values, claims, and institutions—or perhaps to *withdraw* from them insofar as possible? Or did he advise believers to *accommodate* themselves to society insofar as necessary? Did he, like two later New Testament writers, think of believers as *resident aliens* or *sojourners* in this world (1 Pet 2:11; Heb 11:13)? Or did he think of them as still, in some sense, *citizens* of this world who should be concerned for its welfare?

There are passages in five of Paul's letters that shed light on these questions, and we will need to examine each of them in some detail. We begin, however, with a few general comments and observations.

The "Good News" in an Evil Age

As indicated earlier (ch. 1), Paul's expectation that the Lord would soon return to usher in God's kingdom has led many to dismiss his moral instructions as a white elephant—as generally worthless for those who cannot share his belief that the end is near. Along with this, it is often claimed that Paul's view of the world was so negative that it left little room in his thinking for a conception of Christian engagement with the world. According to this assessment, the apostle's moral instructions are properly characterized as *sectarian* because they were meant to help the believing community establish and maintain strictly defined boundaries between itself and society at large.

To be sure, the apostle drew sharp distinctions between *this* age (e.g., 1 Cor 1:20) and the wholly "new creation" in Christ (2 Cor 5:17; Gal 6:15), the latter to be consummated at Christ's return (e.g., 1 Cor 15:24-28). He even described the present as an "evil age" (Gal 1:4) ruled by its own god (2 Cor 4:4); and he regarded everything that belongs to it as "foolish" (1 Cor 1:20; 3:19), condemned (11:32), and doomed to pass away (2:6; 7:31b). We therefore find him issuing appeals like the famous one in Rom 12:2a, "Do not allow yourselves to be conformed to this age" (my translation).

In support of such appeals and in accord with his overall vision of the end, Paul drew sharp moral as well as spiritual distinctions between the Christian community and society in general. He was not content to distinguish merely between "believers" and "unbelievers" (1 Cor 7:12-16; 14:22). Speaking more pointedly, he also distinguished the children of light from the children of darkness (1 Thess 5:5); the blameless and innocent from the crooked and perverse (Phil 2:15); those who know God from those who do not (Gal 4:8-9; 1 Thess 4:5); those who trust and serve God from those who worship idols (1 Thess 1:9-10); those who live by the Spirit of God from those who live by the spirit of the world (1 Cor 2:12); those who have been sanctified from those who remain unrighteous (6:1, 9-11); those who live honorably from those who have succumbed to debauchery and licentiousness (Rom 13:11-13); and those who are being saved from those who are perishing (1 Cor 1:18; 2 Cor 2:15; compare 4:3; Phil 1:28).

If, for these reasons, our topic may seem less than promising, there are other, weightier reasons why it is nonetheless worth pursuing.

1. Most fundamentally, Paul understands the saving purpose of God to be cosmic in scope, inclusive of the whole of humankind and indeed of the whole of creation. He declares, for example, that "in Christ God was reconciling the world to himself" (2 Cor 5:19); and that "the creation itself will be set free from its bondage to decay and will obtain the freedom of the glory of the children of God" (Rom 8:21).

2. Paul summons his converts not to withdraw from society but to live out their faith within it. This is evident not only in his assurance to the Corinthian Christians that he has never meant for them to turn their backs on the world (1 Cor 5:10), but also in many of his specific counsels, as we shall see.

3. In some places Paul specifically encourages believers to include all people within their circle of concern. And in other places he directs them to conduct themselves in ways that outsiders will consider respectable. Our exploration of his letters will bring to light clear and specific instances of both.

Overflowing Love: 1 Thessalonians

The Thessalonian congregation had undergone some kind of suffering, and it was apparently still at risk when Paul wrote the letter that we know as 1 Thessalonians. There is no evidence that the political authorities had targeted the Christians of this city for "persecution." Rather, from the time of their conversion they seem to have experienced discrimination, harassment, insults, and some degree of alienation from their family members, friends, and acquaintances. In Thessalonica, as in the other cities where there were Christian communities, unbelievers perceived the new religion as subversive of traditional social structures and cultural norms. This is important to bear in mind as we consider three significant references to outsiders in 1 Thessalonians.

1 Thessalonians 3:12 and 5:15

Twice in 1 Thessalonians, and using identical phrasing, Paul deliberately expands a reference to believers by adding one to unbelievers. The first occurs in a prayer (3:11-13), which, like many others in Paul's letters, functions partly as an exhortation; what God grants and does, believers are to manifest in their everyday lives. In this case, Paul asks, first, that he be granted a return visit to Thessalonica (v. 11) and, second, that his congregation be enabled to "increase and abound in love for one another and for all" (v. 12). It is the second that commands our present attention. The apostle has already commended the Thessalonians' love (1:3; 3:6), and he will later remark that it is not a subject on which they need to be instructed (4:9). What he prays for here is the *expansion* of their love, not only among themselves but also in their relationships with unbelievers ("for one another *and for all*"). His urging that love be extended beyond the boundaries of the believing community is especially noteworthy because the Thessalonian Christians had suffered much from unbelievers and they continually faced risks and uncertainties in their everyday lives. Under those circumstances, what surer sign could there be of their overflowing love than its extension to outsiders?

Exactly the same expansion occurs in a section of appeals that begins in 1 Thess 5:12. There are appeals that the members of the church should "be at peace among [themselves]" (vv. 12-13); that they should act responsibly in relation to members who are "out of line" (my translation; NRSV has "idlers"), "fainthearted," or "weak" (v. 14); that they should always rejoice, give thanks, and pray (vv. 16-17); and that they should heed the leading of the Spirit as revealed in the words of their prophets (vv. 19-20). But one appeal stands out from these because it is formulated so generally: "See to it that *no one* repays *anyone* evil for evil; instead, *always* strive mightily to do good" (v. 15, my translation). Moreover, using the same wording as in an earlier passage, Paul indicates that this instruction is to be followed not only when dealing with fellow Christians but also when dealing with outsiders: "Strive mightily to do good *for one another and for all*" (italics added). In Paul's letters, "the good" is often synonymous with "love," and that is the case here, where the exact phrase used in 3:12 with reference to love's scope reappears.

In this context, striving to love means, in the first place, not returning evil for evil. Paul is rejecting the law of retaliation ("an eye for an eye, a tooth for a tooth") as it had been set forth in Exod 21:23-25. He is not unique in doing this; the principle had already been questioned within the Jewish tradition itself. But Paul goes farther when he issues the *positive* counsel that one should repay evil with good. This leaves us, however, with two questions. What sense does it make for believers to repay evil with good, even when they have been wronged by unbelievers? And does returning good for evil involve anything more than forgiving the offending party? Another passage in 1 Thessalonians sheds light on these questions.

1 Thessalonians 4:9-12

At the beginning of this paragraph Paul assures the Thessalonians that they "have been taught by God to love one another" (v. 9). It is evident that he regards love as a divine imperative. Then, acknowledging that the Thessalonians already love their fellow believers throughout the rest of Macedonia (v. 10a), he challenges them to "do so more and more" (v. 10b). This call to "overflow" with love echoes both the content and (in Greek) the wording of his prayer for the same in 3:12. Moreover, when he goes on to specify what such love requires, he is clearly urging, once again, that it extend beyond the boundaries of the believing community: the Thessalonians are "to aspire to live quietly, to mind [their] own affairs, and to work with [their] hands . . . so that [they] may behave properly toward outsiders and be dependent on no one" (vv. 11-12). Although interpreters differ on why Paul issued this appeal and what exactly he is urging, several matters that bear on our present topic are clear enough.

1. Certain members of the congregation, having abandoned the employments from which they had been gaining their livelihood, had come to expect support from other believers, or perhaps even from non-Christian relatives and friends. Confronted with this situation, Paul urges them to continue with their usual work in order to be self-supporting (as they knew he himself had been, 2:9-10). Nothing in this paragraph suggests that Paul feared a believer's continuing engagement with society would compromise his or her commitment to the gospel. To the contrary, his directive to continue as responsible members of society seems to reflect his belief that the love that binds them together as believers would thereby be spilling over into their dealings with the unbelieving public.

2. Thus, in this context extending love (practicing "good") toward outsiders means taking responsibility for one's needs without burdening others. Because the Christians in Thessalonica had good reason to feel they had been wronged by outsiders, this counsel requires as its complement the instruction in 5:15 to repay evil with good. In turn, that instruction provides more content to what the "good" is that believers are called to practice in relation to unbelievers.

3. When Paul comments that believers will be conducting themselves "properly toward outsiders" if they follow his counsel (v. 12), he presupposes a certain congruence between the norms that prevail in society at large and the ethos that distinguishes the believing community. He does not mean, however, that believers should try to please outsiders by conforming to what they expect. Rather, they are to "please God . . . more and more" by doing what the "will of God" directs (see 4:1, 3; 5:17). Like all of the entreaties in this letter, the appeal for believers to be responsible members of society derives its significance and urgency from God's having called them "into his own kingdom and glory" (2:12).

"As Though . . . Not": 1 Corinthians

Paul's converts in Corinth seem not to have experienced the kind of marginalization, harassment, and hostility to which Christians in some other places, like Thessalonica, had been subjected. We may suppose that most of them would have readily agreed with Paul that severing all ties with unbelievers was not a realistic option (5:9-10). Clearly, however, they needed help in thinking through how they could remain faithful to the gospel despite their continuing, daily involvement with outsiders. Because much of 1 Corinthians is devoted to providing that help, it also shows us a good deal about Paul's understanding of what it means to be the church in the world. Several passages are especially telling.

1 Corinthians 5:1–6:11

At least some of the Corinthians had understood Paul to say in a previous letter (mentioned in 5:9) that they should separate themselves as much as possible from the world. Paul now denies that, saying that his instruction was to separate themselves from other *believers* who had fallen into immoral practices (5:10-11)—like one of their number who had been sexually involved with his stepmother (the subject of 5:1-13). His comments about this case both presuppose and implicitly reaffirm the significance of the boundary that divides the believing community from society at large. He of course does not counsel believers to withdraw from society, which he acknowledges is impossible anyway; but he also refrains from asking them to limit their contacts with unbelievers, which no doubt would have been possible to some extent. Moreover, he insists that believers should not even stand in judgment of outsiders because that role belongs to God alone (vv. 12-13).

The theme of judgment continues in 1 Cor 6:1-11, where the apostle advises that legal disputes between believers should be settled within the church itself ("before the saints," v. 1), not before civil magistrates (v. 4). In developing his argument, he emphasizes two points about outsider judges. First, they represent and serve within a sphere ("the world," v. 2) to which believers, since they have been transferred into the realm where Christ is Lord (v. 11), are not ultimately accountable. Second, the world itself will be judged by the "saints" (v. 2; here, as in v. 1, Paul's word can be translated, "holy ones"). This may look like a contradiction of what Paul has just said about not judging outsiders (5:12). But now he is thinking of the "final judgment," at which, according to certain traditional Jewish expectations, God's "holy ones" will play a role in judging the unrighteous (e.g., Dan 7:22). Without question, Paul is drawing a very sharp distinction here, but it is not an absolute distinction between the church and the world. It is a distinction between the judgments rendered by civil ("worldly") courts and the judgment of God, to whom believers as well as unbelievers are finally accountable.

1 Corinthians 7:17-24 and 7:29-31

As we have seen (ch. 2), 1 Cor 7 is devoted to questions Paul had been asked about sex and marriage. The apostle's comments in verses 17-24 are intended to support his advice that, if at all possible, those who are married should remain married and those who are unmarried should remain unmarried. Since "the present form of this world is passing away" (v. 31b), believers are not obliged to change their marital circumstances (he offers other examples in vv. 18-23). They are to commit themselves, whatever their place and role in society, to "remain" there *with* God (vv. 20, 24). In this context, remaining with God means keeping God's commandments (v. 19b), and one keeps the commandments by being continually attentive to God's call (v. 17a) and faithful in one's service to Christ, the Lord (v. 22).

Paul returns to the Corinthians' specific questions in verse 25, where he addresses the situation of those who have never been married. While commenting on their situation, he is drawn again into more general remarks about believers in the world:

> The appointed time has grown short; from now on, let even those who have wives be as though they had none, and those who mourn as though they were not mourning, and those who rejoice as though they were not rejoicing, and those who buy as though they had no possessions, and those who deal with the world as though they had no dealings with it. For the present form of this world is passing away. (vv. 29-31)

On a quick reading, it might appear that Paul is now advising believers to withdraw or at least detach themselves from society and their everyday relationships and responsibilities. This, however, is not actually the case.

The apostle's advice here is based on two deep-seated convictions: this age is fast coming to an end (vv. 29a, 31b), and those who belong to Christ must devote themselves as fully as possible to him, undistracted by the claims of the world (see vv. 32-35). Recognizing that these

convictions are framing Paul's outlook helps us understand the "as though
. . . not" statements in verses 29-31a; from his standpoint, one's future is
not with the world but with the Lord. At the same time, however, the
first of those statements—"let even those who have wives be as though
they had none" (v. 29b)—shows that he is *not* advising believers to abandon their present relationships and responsibilities. Given his directive,
in this same context, that marriages, including the physical intimacy of
sexual relations, be maintained, the "as though . . . not" statement about
wives, and therefore all of the others, will have to mean something else.

The last and most general of the "as though . . . not" statements suggests
how all of them are to be understood (v. 31a). Paul directs (I paraphrase, in
part to capture his play on words) that "those who are occupied with everyday responsibilities should not become preoccupied with them." Even
though believers remain in the world, most of them with little or no change
in their social circumstances, their *relationship to* the world has, in Paul's
understanding, profoundly changed. They still have responsibilities in the
world, but those responsibilities no longer define who they are or lay any
ultimate claim on their lives. It is now their belonging to Christ that defines
both who they are and, no less, what it means to "remain with God," whatever the circumstances of their lives and however long this age endures.

1 Corinthians 9:19-23

In chapter 8 Paul has appealed to the more knowledgeable members of
his congregation to avoid eating meat from pagan temples—although he
agrees with them that it is harmless—because doing so could threaten the
faith of the "weaker" members. To support this position, he offers the example of his apostolic practice (ch. 9), emphasizing especially that he has
given up his "right" to a salary in order to make the gospel "free of charge."
In this connection he refers to his missionary principle of accommodation
(vv. 19-23), stating it in two different ways: "[Because] I am free with

respect to all, I have made myself a slave to all, so that I might win more of them. . . . I have become all things to all people, that I might by all means save some" (NRSV, with my alteration). In between these statements he gives three examples of how the principle works. The first two are qualified: in order to "win Jews" he "became *as* one under the law" although he was "*not* under the law" (v. 20, italics added); in order to win Gentiles he "became *as* one outside the law" although he was still "under Christ's law" (v. 21; literally, "in-lawed to Christ"). The third example, to win the weak he "became weak" (v. 22a), is stated without any qualification, perhaps because Paul regards himself as "strong" only by reason of the grace that God has bestowed on him (see, e.g., 1 Cor 2:3; 2 Cor 11:29; 12:9-10).

This missionary principle does not call for capitulation to the values and claims of "the world," whether as represented by Jews and their understanding of the law or by the lawlessness of the Gentiles. It calls, rather, for those who proclaim the gospel to accommodate themselves—*themselves*, not the gospel—to the particular situations and circumstances of those whom they hope to "save." Paul is speaking here of a provisional modification of one's conduct when nothing critical is at stake. For our topic it is especially important that he seems to have regarded this strategy as no less appropriate for believers in their everyday dealings with outsiders. In addition to urging that, if possible, a Christian with an unbelieving spouse stay in the marriage (7:12-16; see above, ch. 2), he accepts it as a matter of course that believers are sometimes dinner guests in the homes of unbelievers (10:27), and that unbelievers are on occasion present for the congregation's worship (14:20-25). In these and many other respects, believers remain involved with the world, even though they are not ultimately subject or accountable to it.

Christians as Citizens: Philippians

In Paul's day Philippi was a city of perhaps ten thousand residents, most of them Roman citizens. Although the religious life of the community was fairly diverse, the imperial cult was especially popular and important. There appears to have been no significant Jewish presence, either in Philippi or in the congregation that Paul established there. Judging from the contents of Paul's letter to this church, the Philippian believers were coming under substantial pressure from the unbelieving citizenry, likely because of their exclusive allegiance to Jesus as "Lord." By rejecting, even if implicitly, the emperor's lordship as celebrated in the imperial cult, believers were opening themselves to the charges of impiety and of being a threat to the political order.

There is no doubt that Paul understood the members of this congregation to be at risk in society, under threat of harassment or worse if they did not conform to its laws and values. Early in his letter he even suggests that their difficulties are part and parcel of his struggle (1:30). Then toward the close of the letter he declares that believers are actually responsible only to a heavenly commonwealth, from which they expect the coming of their "Savior" and "Lord," Jesus Christ (3:20). It is no small thing for Paul to refer here to Jesus as "Savior" and "Lord," for in Philippi, as in other places where the imperial cult flourished, these titles were applied to Caesar. Whether or not Paul intended it, his declaration that believers are under the jurisdiction of a *heavenly* state and look to *Jesus* as their Savior and Lord has a subversive ring. This surely doesn't seem to leave much room for thinking of believers as citizens of the civic community. It is, therefore, all the more significant that such an idea surfaces at several points in this letter.

Philippians 1:27–2:18

Although the appeals in this section of the letter pertain especially to relationships within the congregation (e.g., 2:1-4), the opening and closing appeals pertain to the way believers conduct their lives in the public sphere. The very first one takes account of the opposition that believers face in society:

Only, [conduct yourselves as citizens] in a manner worthy of the gospel of Christ, so that, whether I come and see you or am absent and hear about you, I will know that you are standing firm in one spirit, striving side by side with one mind for the faith of the gospel, and are in no way intimidated by your opponents. For them this is evidence of their destruction, but of your salvation. And this is God's doing. (1:27-28 NRSV, with my alteration)

The key Greek verb here is *politeuesthai*, which means to *be* or *live as a citizen*, and Paul seems to have used it deliberately. It occurs nowhere else in his letters; it is peculiarly appropriate in a letter to believers who reside in a Roman colony and are under pressure to be upstanding citizens; and it coheres with the metaphor of a heavenly "commonwealth" (Greek: *politeuma*), which he also employs only in this letter (3:20). His appeal, therefore, is not just a general one, urging the Philippians to *live their lives* "in a manner worthy of the gospel." The apostle's choice of a recognizably political term points specifically to the *civic, public context* in which believers are called to live in a way that is appropriate to the gospel they have embraced.

It is also significant that Paul has *not* chosen to describe believers as either "resident aliens" or "transients [sojourners]" in Philippi. He would have been well aware that such images had been long applied to Israel (e.g., Gen 23:4); and elsewhere in the New Testament two later writers use them to characterize the status of the Christian community in the world (1 Pet 2:11; compare 1:17; Heb 11:13; compare 13:14). Paul, however, does not call on the Christians of Philippi to conduct themselves as "resident aliens" or "sojourners"; he calls on them to *live as citizens.*" This shows that he endorses some level of participation in civic affairs. Judging from what he says in Romans, specific examples of civic participation would be paying taxes (13:6) and, for anyone with the means and social standing, becoming a public benefactor (doing "what is good," 13:3) and holding public office (16:23). But the apostle's critical point in Phil 1:27 is that believers should fulfill their civic responsibilities "in a manner worthy of the gospel of Christ" as befits persons whose true citizenship is in a heavenly commonwealth.

The appeals in Phil 1:27-30 are carried forward in 2:14-16, where the relation of the believing community to the civic community is again in view.

> Do all things without murmuring and arguing, so that you may be blameless and innocent, children of God without blemish in the midst of a crooked and perverse generation, in which you shine like stars in the world. It is by your holding fast to the word of life that I can boast on the day of Christ that I did not run in vain or labor in vain.

The apostle's concern here is not just that believers be at peace among themselves (v. 14). When he states the aim of his appeal ("so that . . ."), the civic community also comes into view. Although in Deut 32:5 the phrase "perverse and crooked generation" describes disobedient Israel, Paul now applies it to society overall. This is the setting in which they have been called, as God's children, to be "blameless" and "innocent."

Even here, where Paul accentuates the difference between the believing community and the unbelieving public, he does not portray believers as "resident aliens" or "transients" in the world. He now employs a cosmological rather than political image. By conducting themselves as God's children (= under the jurisdiction of a heavenly commonwealth) and "holding fast to the word of life" (v. 16), they will be like the stars that shine in the cosmos. He is summoning believers to be blameless and innocent in *God's* sight, holding fast to the gospel (the "word of life") in spite of the pressures, threats, and hostile actions they may experience from an unbelieving society. He is certainly not urging believers to try to disengage themselves from society. He is encouraging them to stand firm in their faith (compare 1:27) despite the moral darkness of the world in which they presently live.

Philippians 4:5a

After appealing to Euodia and Syntyche to "be of the same mind in the Lord" (4:2-3), Paul offers three general and only loosely related counsels for the congregation as a whole (4:4-6). The second stands out because it is a counsel about how believers should conduct themselves in dealing with others: "Let your gentleness be known to everyone" (v. 5a). In Paul's letters, as throughout the New Testament, the expression here translated as "everyone" almost always refers either to the whole of humankind or to all people with whom one comes into contact. The apostle intends this counsel to apply not only within the believing community but also to the way believers relate to unbelievers. The word translated here as "gentleness" variously connotes kindness, forbearance, mercy, and even forgiveness.

Because Paul offers no specific example, his counsel to show gentleness toward everyone might seem, on the face of it, to be a mere commonplace. It would not have seemed so, however, to the Christians of Philippi, whose lives and livelihood were constantly imperiled by the hostility of the community at large. They would have heard it as a counsel to show moderation, forbearance, and perhaps forgiveness when dealing with unbelievers, including even those who exhibited hostility toward them. In effect, albeit less explicitly, Paul is asking of this congregation what he had previously asked of his congregation in Thessalonica, which was also experiencing the hostility of unbelievers: "See to it that no one repays anyone evil for evil; instead, always strive mightily to do good for one another and for all" (1 Thess 5:15, my translation).

Philippians 4:8-9

Like "gentleness," the qualities and dispositions that Paul mentions in Phil 4:8-9 were recognized throughout the Hellenistic world as benefiting the whole of society, and thus contributing to the common good.

> Finally, beloved, whatever is true, whatever is honorable, whatever is just, whatever is pure, whatever is pleasing, whatever is commendable, if there is any excellence and if there is anything worthy of praise, think about these things. Keep on doing the things that you have learned and received and heard and seen in me, and the God of peace will be with you. (vv. 8-9)

Catalogs of commendable moral qualities and actions are found elsewhere in Paul's letters, but none is so resonant of Hellenistic moral philosophy (especially Stoic thought) as this one. Two of the virtues named appear only here in the New Testament ("whatever is pleasing" and "whatever is commendable"), and two others appear nowhere else in Paul's letters ("whatever is honorable" and "excellence"). Some of the virtues occur rarely or not at all in Paul's Greek Bible, and some that do occur there, or elsewhere in the New Testament, occur in a different form or with a somewhat different meaning.

Unlike his counseling of gentleness toward all people, Paul seems to commend these particular qualities for no specific reason. His list directs the congregation's attention not to special responsibilities that their local circumstances may thrust upon them, but to the broader, public setting in which moral choices have to be made and acted upon. This is the force of the rhetorically powerful, sixfold occurrence of the pronoun "*whatever*" ("whatever is true, whatever is honorable," etc.). Believers are responsible for recognizing and doing *whatever* there is in the world's treasury of wisdom that can be reckoned morally excellent and praiseworthy. Here the apostle is presupposing that at least some of what is esteemed as good conduct in the civic community can be accepted as such also by the believing community.

This is not to say, however, that Paul regards society as itself the *source* of moral insight or ethical norms. His sharp critique of worldly wisdom laid out in 1 Corinthians (1:18–2:16; 3:18-20) is neither softened nor qualified here in Philippians. He is insistent that believers live as citizens who are "worthy of the gospel of Christ" (1:27). For this reason, he follows his commendation of universally recognized virtues like truth and justice with a specific instruction: "Keep on doing the things that you have learned and received and heard and seen in me" (4:9). The congregation has learned, received, and heard from him the gospel of Christ, and it has seen in him what it means to live in accordance with that gospel.

A Time for Doing Good: Galatians

Paul's letter to his churches in Galatia shows that he was deeply troubled by the claim of some that Gentile converts to the gospel should be required to accept and obey the law of Moses. In arguing against this view, the apostle speaks of the freedom that is given with faith in Christ Jesus, and he calls on the Galatians to stand firm against the false teaching that would lead them into slavery to that law (e.g., 2:4; 4:21–5:1).

Paul did not, however, regard freedom from the law as freedom from moral responsibility. He makes this clear in 5:13 through 6:10, a section of directives and exhortations that begins with an admonition about the proper use of one's freedom in Christ: "For you were called to freedom, brothers and sisters; only do not use your freedom as an opportunity for self-indulgence, but through love become slaves to one another" (5:13).

It is possible that Paul formulated some or even most of the subsequent exhortations with the special needs of the Galatian churches in mind. This seems not to be the case, however, with the two general appeals that conclude the section: "Let us not grow weary in doing [the good], for we will reap [in due season, providing we don't give up]. So then, [as we have] opportunity, let us work for the good of all, and especially for those of the [household] of faith" (6:9-10 NRSV, with my alterations).

Theological support for these appeals is given with the promise attached to the first one, that "we will reap [in due season, providing we don't give up]" (v. 9b). This warrant follows logically from Paul's immediately preceding admonition, that those who sow to the flesh "will reap corruption from the flesh," whereas those who sow to the Spirit "will reap eternal life from the Spirit" (v. 8). These two appeals concerning "the good," like all of the pastoral exhortations they bring to a close, presuppose that believers have been graced, through the saving death of the crucified Christ, with the liberating reality of the Spirit's empowering and guiding presence (e.g., Gal 3:1-5; 3:23–4:7; 5:1, 13-25).

The first appeal offers encouragement to persist in doing what is good, and the second emphasizes both the seriousness and the scope of that responsibility. The phrase "so then" introduces an appeal that the apostle deems to be of fundamental importance. The next phrase, "[as we have] opportunity," might seem to suggest otherwise, but it actually lends further weight to the appeal. It does not mean "on whatever occasion may happen to present itself" or "if possible." The key term (*kairos* in Greek) refers to a time that is especially propitious for action. It is the same term that Paul has just used in referring to the eschatological judgment, when it will become clear who has sown to the Spirit and who has sown to the flesh (Gal 6:7-8). Even though he now uses *kairos* of the *present* time, it continues to carry eschatological connotations. For Paul, God's sending of his Son in "the fullness of time" (Gal 4:4) has given to the *whole* of this present time the character of *kairos*—time that has been *claimed* as well as graced by "the promise of the Spirit through faith," which believers have come to know in Christ Jesus (Gal 3:14).

So Paul is not saying, rather generally, "*whenever* we have an opportunity" (NRSV) we should work for the good. He is saying that precisely now, in this "meanwhile" until the Lord's return, in this time that has been graced and claimed by God's promise, believers are to be working for the good. As for the content of this exhortation and its function in this letter, three further observations are in order.

1. "The good" to which believers are summoned is, above all, *love*. Paul begins this section of Galatians by urging that believers use their freedom in Christ for the purpose of serving one another "through love" (5:13). He supports this appeal by declaring that the whole law is fulfilled in the one commandment to "love your neighbor as yourself" (5:14, citing Lev 19:18). And he names love first when listing the fruit of the Spirit (5:22-23). The underlying premise of this whole section, including the call to labor for "the good," is a conviction that Paul expressed earlier: "In Christ Jesus . . . the only thing that counts is faith made effective through love" (5:6, NRSV alternative translation).

2. The exhortation to "work for the good of all" (6:10) has the effect of bringing the preceding counsels out of church and into the public square. Now, sounding more like a Hellenistic moral philosopher than a pastor, Paul speaks simply of *the good*. His use of this all-encompassing and open-ended term suggests that believers are responsible for every conceivable kind of beneficial disposition and deed.

3. Paul's stipulation that believers should work for the good of *all* emphatically broadens his earlier appeal that they serve "one another" through love (5:13). He seems intent on ruling out any interpretation of the love commandment that would require the "neighbor" to be a fellow believer. When he adds that believers should do what is good "*especially* for those of the [household] of faith," he is neither rescinding nor compromising the all-inclusive scope of the appeal. This proviso underscores its urgency by identifying the place where believers

most readily can and therefore most definitely should begin to "work for the good of all."

The Common Good: Romans

In Romans, very likely the latest of Paul's letters, we need to give attention not just to the famous paragraph that refers to governing authorities (13:1-7), but to its context in Romans. Chapters 12 and 13 of this letter constitute a more or less self-contained unit. It opens and closes with appeals that provide an eschatological framework for two groups of counsels that stand in between. The first group pertains to life within the believing community (12:3-13), while the second and larger group pertains to the community's life in society (12:14–13:7).

Romans 12:1-2

Two introductory appeals, which presuppose what Paul has been saying about the gospel up to this point in the letter, lay the groundwork for what follows, especially his counsels about the church's life in the world.

> [Therefore,] I appeal to you, brothers and sisters, by the mercies of God, to [offer up] your bodies as a living sacrifice, holy and acceptable to God, which is your [reasonable] worship. [And do not allow yourselves to be conformed to this age. Rather, allow yourselves to be transformed in the renewal of the mind, so that you can discern] what is the will of God—[the] good and acceptable and perfect. (Rom 12:1-2 NRSV, with my alterations)

The first appeal is stunningly formulated. Using imagery that evokes the rituals of sacrifice as practiced by both Jews and pagans in their holiest places, Paul enlarges the concept of worship to include the believers' "life on the street." Their worship is to consist of the offering of their "bodies," which he describes as "a *living* sacrifice, holy and acceptable to God," their "[reasonable] worship." In Romans, the term *body* stands for the whole self, which in its corporeality and creatureliness (compare "mortal bodies," 6:12) is able to relate to the world and other selves, and which, in Christ, has been set free from the tyranny of sin and death (6:12-13). The "living sacrifice" that is holy and acceptable to God therefore involves putting *oneself* entirely at God's disposal. This kind of worship cannot be confined to special, sacred spaces but must be fulfilled as well in the public sphere, the so-called secular world of the believers' everyday lives.

The second introductory appeal speaks to what is required of the believing community if its worship is to be both "public" in this particular sense and acceptable to God. Although their service of God takes place "on the street," believers must not allow themselves to be conformed to the values, expectations, and claims of this present evil age. Yet the apostle does not call on believers to withdraw from the world (the ascetic option), to form an alternative society (the sectarian option), or to work toward a Christian political order (the theocratic option). Rather, he issues an appeal on the assumption that, for the present, most believers remain involved in the same situation wherein they heard and accepted the gospel (compare 1 Cor 7:17-24). But if their circumstances have not changed, *they* have been changed, and for this reason they no longer belong to the world in the same way as before.

Identifying believers as persons who have been transformed by God and endowed with a "renewed" mind (Rom 12:2), the apostle summons them to the ongoing task of discerning and obeying the will of God. We misunderstand the call to *discern* God's will if we read it as an appeal to "learn" or "be instructed in" a stable body of knowledge (for example, the law; see Rom 2:18). The term that Paul has used points, rather, to a process of inquiry and reflection that includes examining, testing, and appraising whatever may be alleged to be the will of God, or "the good." It is therefore difficult to imagine Paul agreeing with the proposition that "the Bible is the perfect revelation of God's will, including His perfect moral will," or with the inference ordinarily drawn from this, that the scriptural *revelation* renders *critical moral reflection* invalid as well as unnecessary. The apostle's summons is precisely to the task of Christian moral reflection. He calls on believers, as they consider what God requires, to take continuing and careful account of the challenges, the responsibilities, and the opportunities that confront them in the public sphere. Such challenges and responsibilities are the focus of Paul's counsels in 12:14-21 and 13:1-7.

Romans 12:14-21

It is significant that these paragraphs contain no references to Christ or to salvation and that the religious language that does occur (drawn largely from the Jewish Scriptures) was widely understood and appreciated in Greco-Roman society.

> Bless those who persecute you; bless and do not curse them. Rejoice with those who rejoice, weep with those who weep. Live in harmony with one another; do not be haughty, but associate with the lowly; do not claim to be wiser than you are. [Repay no one] evil for evil; take thought for what is noble in the sight of all [people]. If it is possible, so far as it depends on you, live peaceably with all [people]. Beloved, never avenge yourselves, but leave room for the wrath of God; for it is written, "Vengeance is mine, I will repay, says the Lord." No, "if your enemies are hungry, feed them; if they are thirsty, give them something to drink; for by doing this you will heap burning coals on their heads." Do not be overcome by evil, but overcome evil with good. (Rom 12:14-21 NRSV, with my alterations)

The counsels here are only loosely connected and echo various traditions of moral wisdom known to Paul (scriptural, Hellenistic, Hellenistic Jewish). But among these is one appeal that is expressed in a less traditional way than most of the rest and probably explains the aim of the entire paragraph: "If it is possible, so far as it depends on you, live peaceably with all [people]" (v. 18). While "all [people]" would of course include all believers, outsiders are the ones especially in view. The believing community is to maintain amicable relations with the unbelieving public. It is an indication of how seriously Paul intends for this instruction to be taken that he acknowledges the difficulty of accomplishing it— "*if* it is possible." He means, "If it is possible, so far as it depends on *you*." This shows that he is not speaking idealistically but of what believers should try actually to achieve in their dealings even with unbelievers. Behind this conditional clause there also lies, no doubt, the further recognition that what circumstances and other people *do* make possible, or even attractive, may not be in accord with the will of God. To be discerning with respect both to what the circumstances allow and to what is acceptable in the sight of God requires the renewed mind and the commitment to critical inquiry for which Paul has appealed at the beginning of the chapter.

The counsel to try to live peaceably with everyone is complemented by instructions to bless one's persecutors, repay no one evil for evil, and leave vengeance to God (vv. 14, 17a, 19-20). And the paragraph closes with the comprehensive admonition, "Do not be overcome by evil, but overcome evil with good" (v. 21). There are also appeals for sympathy, harmony, and humility (vv. 15-16), which most interpreters read as directed to relationships among believers, but which in this context can just as easily be understood as directed to relationships with outsiders. In either case, Paul is promoting conduct that outsiders could readily observe and would doubtless regard as praiseworthy.

That Paul cares about the church's moral standing in the eyes of the world is evident in his advice, adapted from Prov 3:4 (according to the Greek version), to "give consideration to what is noble in the sight of all people" (v. 17b, my translation). Here again, the apostle assumes some measure of overlap between conduct that is acceptable to God and conduct that is esteemed in society overall. This is even clearer when he quotes the same proverb more fully in 2 Corinthians: "We give consideration to what is noble not only in the sight of the Lord, but also in the sight of people" (8:21, my translation).

Romans 13:1-7

> Let every person be subject to the governing authorities; for there is no authority except from God, and those authorities that exist have been instituted by God. Therefore whoever resists authority resists what God has appointed, and those who resist will incur judgment. For rulers are not a terror to good conduct, but to bad. Do you wish to have no fear of the authority? Then do what is good, and you will receive its approval; for it is God's servant for your good. But if you do what is wrong, you should be afraid, for the authority does not bear the sword in vain! It is the servant of God to execute wrath on the wrongdoer. Therefore one must be subject, not only because of wrath but also because of conscience. For the same reason you also pay taxes, for the authorities are God's servants, busy with this very thing. Pay to all what is due them—taxes to whom taxes are due, revenue to whom revenue is due, respect to whom respect is due, honor to whom honor is due. (Rom 13:1-7)

Unlike the preceding paragraphs, this one is focused on a single topic. The subject here is nothing so abstract as "the nature of the state" but, more concretely, the responsibility of believers—specifically those in Rome—to be good citizens. Paul's advice about fulfilling their obligations as citizens can be understood as following from his earlier, general appeal to try to live peaceably with all people (12:18). Now he indicates that "all people" includes the governing authorities, by which he means local and provincial officials. In dealing with powerful figures like these, the conditions appended to the appeal to strive for cordial relations with everyone—"if it is possible" and "so far as it depends on you" (12:18)—are especially pertinent. The apostle knew this very well from personal experience, which included imprisonments and beatings by local authorities (e.g., Phil 1:12-14; 2 Cor 11:23, 25a). Several particular points in this passage are especially important for our topic.

1. Paul regards the governing authorities as having been instituted by God (Rom 13:1, 4, 6). He understands their authority as *conferred*, not inherent, and he thinks of it as exercised for the specific purpose of supporting the public "good" (vv. 3-4). Here "good" is not an alternative expression for "the will of God," as in 12:2 but refers more specifically to conduct that benefits the wider community (providing, of course, that it accords with God's will). Paul is apparently taking it for granted that the authorities are faithful executors of the will of God, both wise and just in their administration of praise and blame. Despite his difficulties with government officers, he does not pose or consider the question of what would be required of citizens in the event that the ruling authorities were unfaithful to their task of supporting the public good, or unwise or unjust in fulfilling it.

2. The apostle may have something more specific in mind here than simply the responsibility of civic authorities to enforce laws and maintain public order. When speaking of the "praise" that government officers bestow on those who do the good, he employs a term often used in a technical sense of the public recognition accorded to citizens who had in significant ways contributed to the well-being of their city. Moreover, in such contexts the expression "to do the good" meant to perform a notable act of community service. Citizens were officially honored for such acts of

generosity as providing funds for the construction of public buildings, adorning or improving old ones, arranging for relief in times of famine, and contributing to the construction of roads or other public facilities. The apostle's commendation of this kind of public service suggests that he knows (or assumes) that there are some Christians in Rome who have the means to provide civic benefactions on this scale.

3. Paul indicates that believers should be respectful and responsible citizens not just because they fear what will befall them if they are not, but also "because of conscience" (13:5). Although he regards the conscience as a faculty that can be informed by the gospel (see 1 Cor 8:1-13), he certainly does not regard it as a uniquely Christian or even specifically religious capacity. He conceives of it, rather, as the universally human capacity to recognize and reflect on moral claims with some degree of self-awareness, to experience moral obligation, and also to be tormented by moral ambiguity, afflicted by moral shame (the so-called "pangs" of conscience), and uplifted by moral conviction. For example, earlier in Romans he has allowed that when Gentiles "do instinctively what the law requires," they are showing that those requirements are "written on their hearts, to which their own conscience also bears witness" (2:14-15). Accordingly, he now says that subjection to the governing authorities is necessary "not only because of wrath but also because of conscience" (13:5). He is claiming that both believers and unbelievers should be able to recognize, quite apart from what is required by public laws and regulations, that fulfilling the duties of citizenship is a moral obligation ("one *must* be subject," v. 5).

4. For the most part, Paul has constructed and presented this argument for responsible citizenship in a way that could have been understood and affirmed throughout the entire civic community. As in the preceding paragraph (12:14-21), there is no mention of Christ or salvation. The function of the governing authorities is identified in very general terms—

supporting what is good and suppressing what is evil. Good citizens are to be subject to the authorities not only in order to win their praise and avoid punishment but also because their conscience attests that it is "the right thing to do."

5. Although Paul's argument here would have seemed reasonable even to unbelievers, it has a clear theological basis. Believers are to subject themselves to the governing authorities because those authorities are *God's servants* (vv. 4, 6), appointed by God to support the public good. This is why he can call for subjection to the governing authorities even in a passage that he introduces with an appeal *not* to be conformed to this age (12:2). *Conforming* oneself to this age means allowing oneself to be tyrannized by what the world esteems and claims, and that is clearly incompatible with putting oneself wholly at the disposal of God. But *subjecting* oneself to the governing authorities is compatible with serving God insofar as those authorities faithfully discharge their responsibility to be God's agents for the common good. Even so, the subjection that Paul enjoins is provisional in a very profound sense. Like all of the conduct he commends in these chapters, it takes place in the "meanwhile" of this present age. Nothing in this paragraph compromises the apostle's statement in Philippians that believers belong, not just ultimately but even now, to a commonwealth that is in heaven.

There have been times in the history of Christianity when Rom 13:1-7 has been the victim of the sacred-cow view of Scripture. In the 1930s and 1940s, many German Christians cited it as the decisive biblical warrant for obedience to Hitler's Third Reich. During the Vietnam War and the civil rights struggles of the 1960s and 1970s, many American Christians used it against those who advocated civil disobedience. And much more recently, a prominent justice of the United States Supreme Court has read it as calling for unconditional obedience to any "lawfully constituted" government. But in fact, Paul's counsels about citizenship, like all of the counsels in chapters 12–13, are significantly qualified by his introductory and concluding appeals in 12:1-2 (see above) and 13:8-14 (see below). These chapters open and close with powerful reminders that believers are ultimately accountable not to the powers of "this age" but to the God by whose "mercies" (12:1) they have been graced with new life in the "Lord Jesus Christ" (13:14).

Romans 13:8-14

> Owe no one anything, except to love one another; for the one who loves another has fulfilled the law. The commandments, "You shall not commit adultery; You shall not murder; You shall not steal; You shall not covet"; and any other commandment, are summed up in this word, "Love your neighbor as yourself." Love does no wrong to a neighbor; therefore, love is the fulfilling of the law. Besides this, you know what time it is, how it is now the moment for you to wake from sleep. For salvation is nearer to us now than when we became believers; the night is far gone, the day is near. Let us then lay aside the works of darkness and put on the armor of light; let us live honorably as in the day, not in reveling and drunkenness, not in debauchery and licentiousness, not in quarreling and jealousy. Instead, put on the Lord Jesus Christ, and make no provision for the flesh, to gratify its desires. (Rom 13:8-14)

Paul's statements here about love (vv. 8-10) lend a degree of coherence to Rom 12–13 that these chapters would not otherwise have. And his summons to watchfulness in prospect of the approaching end time (vv. 11-14) underscores both the urgency and the provisional character of the conduct that he has commended.

1. When the apostle declares that love is the fulfilling of the law (vv. 8b, 10b), he is saying, in effect, that love is definitive of the will of God, and therefore of the "good and acceptable and perfect" (12:2). Insofar as he gives specific content to the conduct that love requires, it comes in his

quotation of the four commandments, "You shall not commit adultery; You shall not murder; You shall not steal; You shall not covet" (v. 9), and in his own formulation, "Love does no wrong to a neighbor" (v. 10a). The positive counterpart to the latter appears later in Romans: "Each of us must please our neighbor for [the good] of building up the neighbor" (15:2 NRSV, with my alteration).

2. Here as in Galatians (5:13–6:10), the context requires that we understand the command to love "one another" as a command to love *all* others. Paul has just said that *everyone* should be paid *whatever* is owed (v. 7), and this inclusive language continues when he goes on to say that believers should owe *nothing* to *anyone* apart from the continuing obligation to "love one another" (v. 8). Moreover, the Greek word for "neighbor" in v. 9e ("Love your neighbor as yourself," citing Lev 19:18) means *anyone* who is near by, not necessarily a friend or fellow believer. An inclusive interpretation is also more in line with the apostle's earlier counsels about nonretaliation and living peaceably with all (Rom 12:14-21).

3. In 13:11-14 Paul underscores the seriousness with which the Roman Christians should take the moral responsibilities of which he has been speaking. He stresses that the end time is ever nearer (vv. 11-12), and he issues a reminder of the obligations that believers accept at their baptism, when they "put on the Lord Jesus Christ" (v. 14). This is one of only two explicitly christological elements in chapters 12–13 (the other is in 12:5). The appeal to "conduct yourselves honorably as in the day" (v. 13, my translation) is a further instance of Paul's encouraging conduct that outsiders will find commendable (compare 1 Thess 4:12: "Conduct yourselves honorably toward outsiders," my translation). The several dishonorable behaviors he warns about here—reveling, drunkenness, debauchery, licentiousness, quarreling, and jealousy—were regarded as such not only by those who had "put on the Lord Jesus Christ," but also

by Greco-Roman society in general. Once more, believers are being advised, in effect, to "give consideration to what is noble in the sight of all people" (12:17b, my translation).

Observations and Reflections

We have been looking at passages in which Paul spoke, either directly or indirectly, about the church's relation to the world. Our aim was to discover whether the apostle urged believers to withdraw from the world or to accommodate themselves to it. We have discovered, however, no simple answer to this question.

   1. Paul urged believers to understand themselves as ultimately—and already—citizens of a heavenly commonwealth; yet he addressed them as people who were in certain respects still accountable to social and political institutions, and still responsible for contributing to the public good.

   2. Paul's openness to the world is seen in his numerous counsels to maintain, so far as possible, cordial relations with unbelievers; and more than that, to work for their good and embrace them in love.

It is sometimes held that these counsels were motivated by a practical consideration and Paul's missionary goals. Certainly, maintaining good relations with outsiders would increase the opportunities and lower the risks for the church and its members; and a friendly public would be more open to hearing the gospel and, possibly, converting. The practical consideration, however, is evident, if at all, only in 1 Thess 4:12—"so that you may conduct yourselves honorably toward outsiders and be dependent on no one" (my translation). And Paul never even hints that doing good to unbelievers may win them over to the gospel. The linking of humanitarian aid with evangelical outreach that we see practiced by some churches and agencies today has no precedent or warrant in the Pauline letters.

3. The apostle presumed a significant degree of correspondence between what is recognized as "good" by society in general and what may be discerned as "the good and acceptable and perfect" will of God.

He speaks of conduct that will be regarded as "honorable" (Rom 13:13; 1 Thess 4:12) or "noble" (Rom 12:17b; 2 Cor 8:21) in the sight of everyone (compare 1 Cor 5:1; 10:32; Gal 6:10; Phil 4:5a). He directs believers to "test everything" in order to "hold fast to what is good" and "abstain from every form of evil" (1 Thess 5:21-22). He commends *"whatever"* may be affirmed as praiseworthy (Phil 4:8). And he refers to "the [public] good," which governing officials have been authorized by God to serve (Rom 13:3-4). That Paul assumed a certain universal sense of what is good and of what is evil is also clear from his comments about Gentiles, who know "instinctively" and through the witness of their conscience what God requires (Rom 2:14-15; compare 1:20, 32; 13:5).

Such passages do not contradict the apostle's view of the present age as "evil" and doomed to destruction. He did not waver in his belief that God is the source of all good, and that God's love, manifested in the saving work of Christ, is its norm. Nonetheless, and unlike some Christians today, he was not willing to dismiss unbelievers as utterly deprived of moral wisdom and insight, or to assume that believers have nothing to learn from them. For him, the process of Christian moral discernment requires believers to do more than just read their Scriptures, recall their traditions, consult with one another, and wait for the leading of the Holy Spirit. It requires them, as well, to take critical account of whatever society in general deems to be good, just, and honorable, and also of whatever it regards as evil, unjust, and shameful.

4. The stance toward the world that Paul's counsels encourage may be described as critical engagement.

The apostle's eschatological outlook rendered pointless any attempt to "christianize" society (although not the missionary task of carrying the gospel "to more and more people," 2 Cor 4:15), while both practical and theological considerations ruled out the option of *disengagement* from the world (1 Cor 5:9-10; 7:17-24). The choice confronting believers, as he expressed it in Rom 12:1-2, was not *whether* but *how* to conduct their lives in the world. On the one hand, they could allow themselves to be "conformed" to the present age, recaptured by its death-dealing values and claims. On the other hand, as "transformed" persons whose minds had been "renewed" in Christ, they could apply themselves to discerning and doing what God was requiring of them within their present worldly circumstances.

As we have seen, Paul understood that the worldly circumstances of believers included their continuing and sometimes difficult relationships with unbelievers, the intimidation and even hostility that they experienced from the unbelieving public, and constant pressure to fulfill the social and political expectations of the civic community. He did not, however, direct believers to withdraw from their relationships with unbelievers, or categorically to renounce their responsibilities as citizens. Rather, he charged them in all of their dealings with the world to remain faithful to the gospel. This meant embracing whatever they discerned to be in accord with the will of God, rejecting whatever they believed was not, and seeking, as agents of God's love, to "work for the good of all" (Gal 6:10).

We might call this an "interactive" model for the church's moral witness in the world. The believing community is to be a constructive but challenging presence in society, affirming what it can and opposing what it must. As citizens of God's heavenly commonwealth, believers are called, individually and corporately, to the complex and always perilous task of bearing their moral witness precisely where they are caught up in the life of the wider civic community, and doing so as responsible members of society. They are to make the most of every social and political means that may be open to them to oppose whatever does harm and to support whatever contributes to the common good.

Such a course is fraught with many risks, and the apostle called attention to two in particular. On the one hand, the church may so accommodate itself to the world that it compromises the gospel and ceases to be the body of Christ. On the other hand, whenever the church's commitment to the gospel leads it to oppose the world, it may find itself, like Paul, sharing in the sufferings of Christ (e.g., 2 Cor 1:6). Yet that, too, as in the apostle's case, becomes part of its witness (e.g., Phil 1:12-14, 29-30).

5. Paul's encouragement of believers to love and serve one another is often expressed in such a way as to include all people as the beneficiaries.

In making appeals of this type (Rom 13:8-10; Gal 5:13–6:10; 1 Thess 3:12; 5:15) he made no distinction between the uncommon love of God that is constitutive of the believing community, and of which believers are agents in the world, and the love that believers are to extend to outsiders. He commended love toward all people because he understood the whole of humankind to be *already* beneficiaries of the God who "shows no partiality" (Rom 2:11; compare Gal 2:6) and whose love has been "proved" for us "in that while we still were sinners [enemies] Christ died for us" (Rom 5:8, 10).

In short, while the apostle addressed believers as already citizens of a heavenly commonwealth and summoned them to discern and do the will of God, he also counseled them to take seriously their responsibilities as members of society. He called them to recognize that this required their ongoing critical assessment of society's manifold and competing claims about good and evil, right and wrong. And he insisted that what they could determine to be the will of God ought to govern their conduct in relation to society at large no less than their conduct within the believing community.

For Further Reading

I have examined Paul's view of the church in the world at greater length and in more detail in the essay from which this chapter has been adapted, "Uncommon Love and the Common Good: Christians as Citizens in the Letters of Paul," in *In Search of the Common Good* (Theology for the Twenty-first Century; ed. Patrick D. Miller and Dennis P. McCann; New York and London: T & T Clark, 2005), 58–87. See also my essay "Inside Looking Out: Some Pauline Views of the Unbelieving Public," in *Pauline Conversations in Context: Essays in Honor of Calvin J. Roetzel* (Journal for the Study of the New Testament, Supplement Series 222; ed. Janice Capel Anderson, Philip Sellew, and Claudia Setzer; Sheffield: Academic Press, 2002), 104–24.

Quotations in this chapter: the statement referring to the Bible as the "perfect revelation of God's will" is in a resolution adopted by the Southern Baptist Convention in June of 1996 that called for the prohibition of partial-birth abortions. The claim that Rom 13:1-7 speaks of "unconditional obedience" is made by Antonin Scalia, "God's Justice and Ours," *First Things* 123 (May 2002): 18–19.

Studies that bear on matters discussed in this chapter: David Horrell, "Ethics and Outsiders," in *Solidarity and Difference* (listed with the "Further Reading" at the end of ch. 1), 246–72. More detailed: Bruce W. Winter, *Seek the Welfare of the City: Christians as Benefactors and Citizens* (First-Century Christians in the Graeco-Roman World 1; Grand Rapids: Eerdmans, 1994); Craig Steven de Vos, *Church and Community Conflicts: The Relationships of the Thessalonian, Corinthian, and Philippian Churches with Their Wider Civic Communities* (SBL Dissertation Series 168; Atlanta: Scholars Press, 1999); Mikael Tellbe, *Paul between Synagogue and State: Christians, Jews, and Civic Authorities in 1 Thessalonians, Romans, and Philippians* (Coniectanea Biblica, New Testament Series 34; Stockholm: Almqvist and Wiksell, 2001).

Commentaries on 1 Corinthians, Romans, and Galatians are listed, respectively, with the "Further Reading" for chapters 2, 3, and 4. For Romans, see also Ernst Käsemann, "Worship and Everyday Life: A Note on Romans 12," and "Principles of the Interpretation of Romans 13," in *New Testament Questions of Today* (Philadelphia: Fortress, 1969), 188–216.

Commentaries on 1 Thessalonians: Victor Paul Furnish, *1 Thessalonians, 2 Thessalonians* (Abingdon New Testament Commentaries; Nashville: Abingdon Press, 2007); Beverly Roberts Gaventa, *First and Second Thessalonians* (Interpretation; Louisville: John Knox, 2000); Abraham Smith, "1 Thessalonians: Introduction, Commentary, and Reflections," in *The New Interpreter's Bible* 11 (ed. L. E. Keck et al.; Nashville: Abingdon Press, 2000), 671–737. More detailed: Abraham J. Malherbe, *The Letters to the Thessalonians: A New Translation with Introduction and Commentary* (Anchor Bible 32B; New York: Doubleday, 2000).

Commentaries on Philippians: Morna D. Hooker, "Philippians: Introduction, Commentary, and Reflections," in *The New Interpreter's Bible* 11 (ed. L. E. Keck et al.; Nashville: Abingdon Press, 2000), 467–549; Carolyn Osiek, *Philippians, Philemon* (Abingdon New Testament Commentaries; Nashville: Abingdon Press, 2000). More detailed: Gordon D. Fee, *Paul's Letter to the Philippians* (New International Commentary on the New Testament; Grand Rapids: Eerdmans, 1995).

INDEX OF REFERENCES

Old Testament

Apocrypha

Other Jewish Writings

New Testament

Other Ancient Greek and Latin Works